AWA PRESS
Old Bucky & Me

'Essential reading'
Lonely Planet New Zealand 2012

'An intelligent, articulate and moving record of one
of the major events in our history'
North & South

'Wry, witty and wonderfully observant, immune to bullshit
and platitudes, conveying the fullest sense of life amid the 'muntage'
away from orange-jacketed press conferences'
Listener

'Quite simply a remarkable contemporary record of a major
event in New Zealand's history'
The Waikato Times

'An entertaining read with wry observational humour and insight of what it
was like to be in Christchurch during this time … A great read not only for
those from Christchurch, but more importantly for those from elsewhere
around the country who are wondering just what life was like after the
quake and also why most of the city chose to stay'
Tomorrow's Schools Today

'Bowron hits just the right note. She doesn't big-note emotionally but the
pain, bewilderment and determination to keep going are all there'
Peter Wells

'Colourful and amusing, yet totally real and honest … this book
will be a record to hand on to future generations to help them
appreciate what we've all been through'
*Ruth's Reflections: Observations on life
in inner-city Christchurch and elsewhere*

'Brilliantly written'
Te Awamutu Courier

Jane Bowron is a freelance journalist based in Christchurch, New Zealand. She is currently a television reviewer for *The Dominion Post* and a columnist for *The Dominion Post* and *The Press*. Her extensive career includes feature writing for *The Sunday Star-Times* and television reviewing for *The Evening Post*, *The Sunday Star-Times*, National Radio *Nine to Noon*, Radio Live and NewstalkZB. She has been a media commentator for NewstalkZB and has published a collection of poetry, *Scenes Away from the Crime*.

JANE BOWRON
OLD BUCKY & ME

DISPATCHES FROM THE CHRISTCHURCH EARTHQUAKE

FOREWORD BY
PAULINE O'REGAN

AWA PRESS

Second edition published in 2012 by Awa Press,
Level One, 85 Victoria Street,
Wellington, New Zealand.

Copyright © Jane Bowron 2011

Columns in this book originally appeared in
The Dominion Post and *The Press*. This edition includes 26 new
columns not included in the first edition published in 2011,
ISBN 978-1-877551-30-7.

The right of Jane Bowron to be identified as the author
of this work in terms of Section 96 of the Copyright Act 1994
is hereby asserted.

Photographs courtesy of Fairfax Media New Zealand.

This book is sold subject to the condition that it shall not, by
way of trade or otherwise, be lent, resold, hired out or otherwise
circulated without the publisher's prior consent in any form
of binding or cover other than that in which it is published
and without a similar condition including this condition being
imposed on the subsequent purchaser.

Bowron, Jane, 1958-
Old Bucky & me : dispatches from the Christchurch earthquake /
Jane Bowron ; foreword by Pauline O'Regan. 2nd ed.
Previous ed.: 2011.
ISBN 978-1-877551-40-6
1. Bowron, Jane, 1958- 2. Christchurch Earthquake, N.Z., 2011
--Personal narratives. 3. Earthquakes—Social aspects—New
Zealand—Christchurch. I. Dominion Post (Wellington, N.Z.) II.
Press (Christchurch, N.Z.) III. Title.

This book is typeset in Minion Pro and Helvetica Neue
Typesetting by Tina Delceg
Printed by Midas Printing International Ltd, China

www.awapress.com

To the Aged Parents –
no longer here but always here

Acknowledgements

Many thanks to Slim Laws for archiving the columns; Awa Press for the idea for this book; *The Dominion Post* and *The Press* for allowing it to happen; Pauline O'Regan for the wonderful foreword; the backyard gang and the garage people for the camaraderie; Benecio for getting me through; and most of all the people of Christchurch, who keep on putting one foot in front of the other.

Jane Bowron

Contents

Foreword	1
Riding the cycle of life and death	4
Move over, *Survivor*	9
Unwashed supermodels	13
Forbidden city	16
No place for a lady	19
Company	23
Cabin fever	26
Italianate gestures	30
Barney Rubble	34
The postman cometh	37
Speaking in tongues	40
Life in Eastern Europe	43
Jerk patrol	46
The new normal	49
Mars might be nice	52
Rough trade	55
Friends and neighbours	59
Crescendos of collapse	63
Goodbye to the republic	66

Bless this house	69
A bloody good cat	72
Returning to brick city	75
The kindness of strangers	79
Unpeopled park	83
Quake porn	87
City of once	92
Orderly swilling	96
Anger management	100
Noses	105
Nine lives	110
A short history of tractors	115
Tumbleweed days	119
The whites of our eyes	124
Waiting for Gerry	128
Deep freeze	133
Cracking up	138
Life in the fridge	143
Stepping up to the plates	148
Briefly Russian	153
Taking care of business	157
The all shook up future	161
Snow falling on ruins	166
Learning to swim	170
Our own 9/4	174

Mall life	178
Funkytown museum	182
In the spirit	186
Marching orders	190
Love and loathing in the dunes	194
Exposing oneself	198
The new chic	202
High visibility	206
Revelations	210
Piggy and other bad dreams	213
The last goodbye	217
Summer on the grass	221
Sporting red	224
Nativity scenes	227
More skew-whiffery	231
Indomitability	234
Entrepreneurs	238
In the belly of the whale	241
Happy hour	245
Life after people	248
Revolting peasants	252
Coffee klatches	256
A chance to find the sunshine	259

Foreword

As I read these daily accounts of life in Christchurch during and after the February earthquake, I found myself going through waves of unexpected emotion. As they say in the best psychological terms, they 'triggered' emotions in me that I had scarcely known were there. After all, I live in Christchurch and I had also survived the quake – quite well, I was inclined to think – so I should have known what to expect. We all like to imagine we are in touch with our inner feelings, so my too-ready tears and bursts of slightly hysterical laughter seemed to call for an explanation. I had to ask what there was about Jane Bowron's writing that had affected me so deeply.

In the end I decided it was the immediacy of these accounts, the integrity, the honesty, the hitting-the-nail-on-the-head quality of them that had got to me. I feel sure that as Jane met the unforgiving deadline of a daily newspaper, she must have written these pieces at night, exactly as they had happened that same day. She tells us she is an insomniac

Foreword

and so I picture her sitting up in bed, writing, body on full alert for the next heart-racing aftershock, recalling the extraordinary events of the day just gone and recording them just as they happened, with no time for rueful adjustment or careful rewriting. You don't get writing more immediate than that – and this writing is immediate and compelling.

I can't help feeling this is the way Samuel Pepys wrote his diary: late at night, desperate to get everything down within the limitations of a single page, telling it exactly as he experienced it that very day, urgently, immediately, honestly. That is surely the kind of pressure under which he recorded the terrible events surrounding the Great Fire of London in 1666 that destroyed his beloved city. Like Jane Bowron's earthquake of 2011, the fire was too terrible an event in itself to allow for any embellishment in the writing, too life-threatening to tolerate histrionics, too innately dramatic to need dramatic prose. So what we got from Pepys was a true, unadorned account of a great event in history, couched in good plain English. Jane Bowron has done no less.

I like to think that in these accounts of a great and terrible event in her lifetime, Jane has done for Christchurch what Samuel Pepys did for London. Both cities were destroyed by forces beyond human control, both writers were living in the heart of the city at the time, both loved their city dearly, and both conveyed without self-pity or excess of words that their hearts were broken.

I don't know what it has cost Jane in emotional and physical burn-out to write these accounts of the Christchurch earthquake, but I want her to know that she has done all of us a huge service. I experienced the quake and its aftermath in a city suburb. What I have lived through may not have all the intensity of her experience, living as she did in the inner city, 'within the cordon', but it has taken me to the limit of my endurance all the same. In this book, Jane has told my story and I am very grateful to her. I believe she has told the story of everyone in Christchurch who has experienced these events. And what is really heart-warming is that these stories were published first in a Wellington newspaper, and were received and valued by its readers, who were obviously interested in what we in Christchurch were going through and were concerned for our welfare. We needed that demonstration of solidarity and we drew courage from it.

Most of all, I believe this book will be important to generations to come. It will still be on bookshelves far into this century and grandparents will take it down and say to the children of the future: *There was a terrible earthquake in Christchurch on February 22, 2011 and this is what happened...*

Pauline O'Regan
August 2011

Riding the cycle of life and death

FEBRUARY 24 – When the big aftershock of last year's earthquake struck on Boxing Day, a friend texted, 'So God isn't happy with his presents then?' After this Tuesday's earthquake it seems He doesn't like his churches very much either.

When the quake struck I was sitting in a café, one of a group of 'alternative' shops on the corner of Barbadoes and Kilmore Streets. People know the corner because of the Piko Wholefoods' building, which is made of brick. Everyone marvelled when that building withstood the September quake, but on Tuesday at lunchtime it fell – to become, like so many other broken buildings, a symbol of the architecture of suffering.

The café next door, where I was, is made of iron, so when the quake hit I, like the rest of the occupants, tried to get out of my chair and move to the door. A young mother pushed, nearly threw, a baby into my arms so she could walk across the road to her car to get her cellphone. I stood in the middle of the road with this tiny baby as the building opposite fell to the ground and the owner miraculously sidestepped out of it.

All around, buildings started to deconstruct themselves into dolls' houses with their sides off. In a matter of seconds the alternative shops of the Avon Loop had been wiped out, closed for business. People wept, embraced. I remember I kept saying, 'We're alive, we're alive' as we all came to the unspoken collective conclusion that this quake had been sent to cure us of any amnesia about last year's September 4 quake and its horrid intent.

My flat was four doors away. After the mother was reunited with her baby I stumbled home to see that the two chimneys, which had been examined by the Earthquake Commission and approved three weeks previously, had taken aim and collapsed on my new Suzuki. It's not so swift now. Inside the flat there was the usual fury of thrown objects, everything smashed and covered with an unguent of oil, coated with flour.

Miriam, my neighbour, arrived and we packed backpacks full of towels and bandages, pills and any first aid we could find and walked intuitively to Latimer Square, an al fresco assembly point. At the far end, off-duty nurses were swiftly and efficiently tending to the injured while helicopters dropped first-aid kits. We left our contributions, assessing we would be more hindrance than help, and tried to comfort the elderly and bewildered.

Beyond Latimer Square, Madras Street was a mess of smoke, collapsed buildings, fire and panic. Yellow-jacketed emergency workers stood in a frozen tableau outside the CTV building like something seen on 9/11 footage. I had to check out Holy Trinity, the church where my brother is vicar, a historic church that is the oldest in Christchurch. When we came to the intersection of Kilmore Street and Fitzgerald Avenue the road became increasingly buckled. The bridge across the Avon looked precarious to say the least, and the traffic was gridlocked. Cars were packed with whatever the drivers could take to get out of Dodge as fast as possible. Other people were trying to leave their houses and join the line.

My brother's church, badly hit on September 4, now barely had anything left standing. The marble orchard that surrounds the old stone beauty was littered with shattered ancient headstones; the lounge where temporary services had been held had collapsed. The intellectually handicapped people who live in assisted housing in a building backing on to the lounge were sitting in a forlorn but orderly line on the church gate. Everyone had got out, they said, and gave a cheerful thumbs up.

Back at my flat, people in our house and the one next door, each containing six flats, came together. We pooled whatever we had – water, gas cooker, food, wine – and managed to get a hot meal together. Introductions were made, people told each other where their kith and kin were, where they had been when the quake struck. The rain came and the nearly all-female group sorted out tarpaulins, dug a toilet in the garden, and got busy with the necessities of life.

No one wanted to go back inside and do the rough-Cook-Strait-ferry-crossing walk as the huge aftershocks, much bigger than September 4's, hit again and again. I slept half inside, half out, in a garage we cleared for communal living.

As soon as dawn inched in I took tea to the intersection, where three volunteers had been directing traffic for fourteen hours. When it seemed that the aftershocks, the worst of which had struck about three a.m., were abating I got on my bike and cycled down Kilmore Street to see the devastation. At the corner of Colombo and Kilmore the quaint old Johnson's Grocery Store, the Whisky Shop and the Bodhi Tree restaurant were blasted away, only frames standing. Turning into Park Terrace, I navigated the humps and holes everywhere in the road, noting that the museum was cordoned off and that Christ's College, despite all the money an old boy could throw at it, had taken a hit.

When I got to the Bridge of Remembrance, the base of which looked fragile, I could see that Cashel Street, badly hit on Boxing Day, looked sore and ominous. Officials waved me back, saying, 'You don't want to be going in there – it's dreadful.' Every inner-city corner was cordoned off, with a heavy presence of light armoured vehicles; soldiers were poking out the tops, watching for looters. From a distance I saw that the Catholic Cathedral was missing one dome.

Speeding down Barbadoes Street, I came across a man walking down the middle of the road clutching a pharmaceutical bag for dear life. 'You okay, mate?' I asked. He looked right through me, his eyes barmy with shock. When I got to the cathedral, the building upon which George Bernard Shaw had lavished so much praise was quite humbled: at the front all that was left was a cross piercing the sky, with two angels abreast keeping vigil.

Glances down side streets into the troubled, hurt core showed ambulances waiting to bring out the trapped and buried. Yesterday, choppers had beat their way across Kilmore Street to the Avon River, where their monsoon buckets had artfully scooped up water to dowse the fire raging at the CTV building. The ducks loved it; one had even got scooped up before flying off. Next day the helicopters returned, no buckets this time, just a feeling we are being watched. Last night tanks rolled down our street and trained their lights into our houses.

There is a feeling of massive disconnect but we have formed a unit, and even though we are cordoned off within the four avenues we know the priority is to liberate those trapped. We feel helpless – we cannot help – but we are helping each other, waiting for power, plumbing, civilisation, a far-off ambition perhaps but something to aim for.

Move over, *Survivor*

FEBRUARY 25 – Wonderful news. Miriam and I had just returned from a sortie out on the bikes to get wine from a liquor store operating out of a darkened doorway, where the owner was using a wheelie bin for a counter and doing strictly cash transactions, when the landlord greeted me with the fantastic news that 'Vesuvius' had turned up.

What? I asked, realising a split second later that he meant my cat Benecio, who hadn't been seen since the quake. Benecio was skinny, frightened and limping badly, indicating his injury might be spinal. It goes without saying that you can't get a vet for love or money in this town, and time is the only healer available. He couldn't jump up on the bed, so we slept on the floor next to each other, and I swear he kept a purr up for two hours non-stop.

The aftershocks through the night had a mean kick to them, and dawn couldn't arrive fast enough for us to start getting on with this new life we have all found ourselves in. I saddled up and biked to the corner of Park Terrace and Bealey Ave, where the army boys were dishing out free bottles of water. When I got back, Mark, who's got God in a big way, was the only one up and we set to stringing up a tarpaulin at an angle, with pots at the end to collect rainwater. Mark informed me that God was bringing rain on Friday and, because of this divine deliverance, could he ask that I and the others refrain from using His name in vain.

The presumption that somebody else's god is the sole arbiter of our fate is an arrogance to those of us who believe the human spirit will get us through. 'I suppose Satan was responsible for Tuesday's twitch,' I was on the brink of saying, but bit my lip, knowing Mark and I could be spending serious time together. Tolerance, tolerance, I thought, as we set about using the bricks that had fallen from the chimneys to build an old-style barbecue, and stashed whatever wood we could find in the back of the garage. Move over, *Survivor*, you've got nothing on us.

My flat is inside the cordon surrounding the CBD and getting in and out of the cordon is proving more and more difficult. Army personnel wave you down and ask for ID, which seems completely nonsensical. Ask them questions about supermarkets or eftpos machines nearby that might be open and they look blankly at you and say, 'Don't ask me, love, I just got here two hours ago from Nelson … or Dunedin' … or wherever.

Christchurch has turned into an army town teeming with men in uniform blocking off streets, and two firemen turned up at the hacienda yesterday to see if we had a pulse, nodding approvingly at our set-up.

On every street you see sad bunches of people carrying sleeping bags, pillows, whatever they can, as they trudge towards the nearest shelter. Talk to them and they tell the same story. They are tired and beaten from long nights of aftershocks; the fear has set in and they need the comfort of the herd.

Yesterday, a dodgy-looking guy waved me down and asked if I knew where an operating toilet was, to which I replied, 'Haven't you dug a hole in the backyard?'

'Not yet,' he said, asking if he could use ours, and I know this sounds mean-spirited but I said no. I didn't want him casing our joint, and he was a great big lug who would fill our earth toilet with his enormous deposit. This is how you think.

Three doors down from us dwells a house of complete hard cases. There is a puce-faced old guy with a gut on him like a Taranaki bull, a woman nursing cracked ribs from the quake, and a younger dude with all his front teeth missing – and not from the quake. They always crack a good chat, and at nine in the morning were chugging back tinnies and asked if I wanted one. A wee bit early for me, I said, adding that if one weren't an alcoholic after September 4 you were one now.

We were running low on gas cylinders and I asked them if they had found a shop open in their travels that might sell such a thing. Next thing a cupboard was unlocked and they were pressing gas cylinders into my arms, saying pay us back later. Turned out their barbecue gas bottle was out and I had a spare one with no barbie, so we did a contra deal, which was great because everyone is running low on cash.

Never thought I'd find myself pining for an eftpos machine. But you know what I miss most? Washing. I'd kill for a hot shower or a cleansing dip in the sea. Electricity isn't coming for weeks to the central city, rumour has it, and cordons keep us from the ocean.

The landline is up and you find yourself doing mini press conferences to friends and relatives who want to Stevie Wonder you ('I just called to say how much I care') and seek an update.

It is maddening for those living here being told by outsiders how our city looks in the television footage. It is particularly frustrating for a TV reviewer with a non-performing television. I suppose there is a lesson in all this. Perhaps it is the opposite of the one learned by the three little pigs – that is, don't build your house out of bricks.

Unwashed supermodels

FEBRUARY 26 – This morning I ventured over to Richmond to try and visit a friend in Hills Road but had to turn back because the liquefaction was waist-high. You see people cycling around with shovels poking out of the back of their bikes to lend a hand where they can.

On my way I saw a park bench of people feasting on fish and chips and yelled out, 'They look good!' which prompted an invitation to join them. I'm a sucker for a hot chip. I slammed on the brakes and asked a woman about my age with dreadlocks where she was on Tuesday and what she did for a living. She said she was a counsellor specialising in post-earthquake trauma. I had to laugh.

Yesterday it was sunny, turning the liquefaction into sand that blew in our eyes and hair and made everybody a dusty shade of cowboy brown. Today, as predicted by the Christian in our group, God has brought rain and the water has come back on. There's no power but we have an outdoor brick fire going like the clappers 24/7 and I am going to have a half-inch bath.

This morning I saw a lovely young couple sitting out in front of their house with a sign that said 'We can rebuild'. Bored with sitting inside and staring at the four walls, they had turned their liquefaction into a beautiful sandcastle city using beer-bottle tops for the windows of houses. 'It gives everyone a smile,' they said. 'Even the police didn't tell us off for drinking on the street. They said, "Good on you."'

At the corner of my street the volunteer traffic directors have brought old chairs and a guitar and are having a good old singalong.

Each day the cordoned area of the four avenues, where I live, seems increasingly deserted. When someone goes out and comes back in they have to debrief on where they've been and what they've seen. That is our television. Everyone brings what they can – pears and plums from trees, tools, funny stories, and acts of kindness. Our survival unit has now swelled to seven with two young guys from two doors down who lost the sides of their house. They brought their possessions across to us and we try to squeeze as much of it as we can into our home.

We are getting fit from all the walking and biking, and talk about looking like unwashed supermodels… Living in the avenues of the cordon, we have to get our to-ing and fro-ing done before the six-thirty curfew that's in place until seven next morning. We wish the Iroquois helicopters would cease and desist – they are supposed to keep away from the city centre so if the buried are still alive the rescuers can hear them tapping.

Benecio, my cat, has gone missing again. I am trying not to think about that. And as the end of the day approaches, my home is yellow-stickered. That means I need to find somewhere else to live. I try not to think about that either.

Forbidden city

MARCH 1 – It has been quite a weekend. Benecio turned up on Saturday limping very badly. I put him in the cage, got in my munted car and Mad Maxed it the wrong way up Barbadoes Street with a smashed windscreen and dangling side mirrors. Arriving at the cordon, I grabbed the cage and cat, produced two kinds of ID and jumped into a friend's car that was hovering to spirit us away to the vet's. We had twenty minutes to get there before it closed and just made it, weaving around the streets madly to find a way through. On arrival, Benecio was given a shot of morphine and will have to have two procedures to get him back on his feet. But at least he's safe.

Our community, which numbered seven, was four over the weekend and is now down to three. Miriam has been sleeping in the lounge with me for the last two nights and we go over what we have achieved in the day and what we should aim for tomorrow. The home fires are kept burning all day, heating a preserving pan full of water, because we are still without power.

On Sunday I set off for Bunnings in Blenheim Road – a big haul on the bike – for batteries, a camp shower and small gas cylinders, which they were out of. On the long way back I got lost in the inner cordon, and my god it was eerie in there. I biked up Peterborough and Salisbury Streets around Cranmer Square and saw only one civilian in twenty-five minutes. There are hardly any of us left and everyone has quit the inner city.

On Sunday, Civil Defence turned up in our street and came through checking every building for signs of life, death and looters. Those who fled the city locked their doors, which are now being broken down. A chap we call Vincent because he does Van Gogh-like paintings and has blood-nut red hair was visiting his girlfriend in Brighton when they came to his house. We told Civil Defence we had seen him only hours before, but no, once again they had been given their orders to break and enter. All very well, but now the whole street is ripe for looters.

Then the army came through our property looking for a burglar. They noted the yellow stickers on the doors – which means 'enter at your own risk' – and frog-marched one of our number out of the cordoned area. He had to sleep in his car. This morning he was sitting around the campfire, having got back in, with a story to tell. Even though we have a yellow sticker, late on Friday two firemen told us our building was safe. We wait for a green sticker to give us power.

The curfew is stricter than strict. Yesterday morning, if you went out you couldn't get back in for a couple of hours. And you can't leave your house after six-thirty at night without attracting a rushing military vehicle. God knows what will happen with all this unsecured property if they suddenly remove the army.

I sleep clothed, with a baseball bat. Another girl, Millie, and I have agreed that if some of the dodgy blokes up the way ask questions, we will tell them we have a lot of men living here.

To get to the supermarket I have to go down Stanmore Road, which has an endless line of dusty third-world traffic that never diminishes. The service station is always snaked about with long lines of cars, whose drivers want gas cylinder bottles filled. Inside the supermarket, tellers wear masks.

'Is that for the dust or the smell of the patrons?' I ask.

'Both,' they say, looking at the more feral, crazed customers.

There is a definite feeling of every man for himself as you get from the emptying shelves what you can carry in a backpack. Six-thirty p.m. comes quickly. There's so much to do and organise that it usually goes wrong and we have all had a crack-up.

While Benecio is on hold at the vet's, Toby and Sue are coming back more and more to camp. I tell Millie that they're getting more human by the day, or perhaps it's just that we are becoming more feral.

No place for a lady

MARCH 2 – The very gratifying latest is that on Monday afternoon both our households were reclassified with the coveted green stickers after yet another team came through, evaluating our dwellings for structural integrity. Millie and I begged and pleaded with them and after much deliberation they gave us the green light, the perpetrator of the sacred document refusing offers of a hug from a couple of filthy ferals.

We broke out the vino, Vincent climbed over the fence from next door with a couple of guitars and gallon jars, and we partied like there was no tomorrow. Even the devout Christian allowed himself a small tipple. He has done Trojan work in the camp, helping out the builders next door to his flat so they could brace the house, thus giving his own gaff a green sticker, and quietly does his share, demonstrating that he is a weight-puller. As we speak the electricity inspectors have just this minute arrived to work their magic, and lo and behold there is light.

I slammed the washing machine on, feeling how strange it was that only this morning after dawn's crack I had risen early and started the fire to boil enough water for the meanest of baths.

I had to get the car to the assessor and drove Mr Suzuki Swift gingerly out to a semi-industrial area normally a short five minutes drive away. It took me over two hours to get there, taking a labyrinthine path. The mechanics got terribly excited about Mr Swift's damage and wanted to know what had caused such impressive 'muntage' – the new post-quake word on the street. They even gave me a replacement dunger. It is very low slung in the undercarriage and I nearly did it a mischief driving over the hillocks of liquefaction.

I called in on the hard-case Garage People, as they are now known, to show them my machine. They had just taken Lorraine out to Rangiora to her daughter's. They nodded philosophically, 'Best off there. This is no place for a lady,' but boy, they do seem quite lost without her.

There are definitely fewer of us here within the cordon, but now that the power is back on life seems so much more doable. Along Stanmore Road the traffic continues to inch as trucks pass through, spraying water to damp the dust of liquefaction down before threatened gales blow up tonight. I went and sat down on a park bench with two old codgers who, if they weren't tramps before, look like them now. Charlie said he lived in the inner CBD. All his clothes are in there, if there is anything there that still stands, and he can't get back in. All he had to his name was a blue cloth shopping bag and he had to make it way back across town to the Burnside shelter before nightfall. Means of transport? Shanks' pony, he told me, refusing an offer for food or cash before limping off across the park. My god, it was sad to see him go like that.

Inside the supermarket the noticeboard bears photos of what looks like Japanese students under a 'Missing' headline. At 12.51 p.m., exactly one week after the quake hit, the crass supermarket music stopped, a lady asked us to observe two minutes' silence for the people of Canterbury, and everybody stopped what they were doing mid flow. We stood gravely still, looking like those street theatre entertainers who paint their bodies statue-grey then freeze-pose.

On the way home I stopped at a greasies' shop and ordered fish and chips for a treat, realising after being out and about that the mood has changed. People aren't spontaneously greeting each other so much any more. They stare into the middle distance, trying to shock-absorb, arrange their losses, and bottom-line themselves. If this isn't the look of post-traumatic stress syndrome I don't know what is.

Back at base, texts have been sent out that the sparkies have been and everyone is trickling back, vowing to keep the backyard gang going and have a barbie over the fire every once in a while. We all know each other now, we keep saying, in some amazement at how we have been thrown off the deep end and come to grips with strangers over the last few days. Some are angry at the way their employers have abandoned them and not given any indication about when work will begin again, or even asked if they are alive, while others are too traumatised to return to big buildings to relive the moment.

Tonight I'll try and get the TV up and running but I'm not holding my breath. I wonder what it will feel like to see my first images of what went down in this town only a week ago.

Company

MARCH 3 – On Tuesday night I called in to see the padre, my brother Hugh, and was having a debrief about the whereabouts of our Christchurch-dwelling family when suddenly I looked at my watch and it was five minutes to curfew. I flew on to the bike and pedalled madly to the border, where the militia gave me a thoroughly good ticking off for cutting it fine.

On the corner of Kilmore Street and Fitzgerald Avenue is a brick pub called Pomeroy's, which still stands. Next door is a charming cottage which, until the day of the quake, operated as boutique accommodation. The Pomeroy family have been living there since their house got munted in Cashmere. I knew Mrs Pomeroy in a former life, when we knocked around together in the Avon Loop and she was the queen of the hippies. As I cycled past she beckoned me in and invited me to have a curfew cocktail. Initially I declined because I might not be allowed back into my house.

'Don't worry, you can park up here if they won't let you back in,' she said.

So I stopped a while and was given two very generous gins, so stiff I would call them erect. We swapped stories and had a laugh about the building in Fitzgerald Avenue that has all but collapsed bar the framework, exposing two enormous marijuana plants, which sit brazenly in their pots, imperiously surveying the work going on to the massively damaged avenue.

I managed to get home and sat up with Millie and talked, mostly about the marvels of electricity. BC the power being on I was writing these dispatches in long hand and dictating them down the phone, so it is fantastic to be back on the keyboard. The television's kicked the bucket though, so no images yet of the carnage.

The people of Christchurch still keep leaving in droves but I have discovered another woman, Kirsty, remaining on the street with a friendly dog named Chloe. Kirsty was thrilled to have gone online yesterday morning and seen her bank balance go from six bucks to five hundred and sixty, so Work and Income is on to it. Before the quake, Kirsty's livelihood was teaching archery so I told her I'd be sticking with the bow-and-arrow lady; if things get ugly she can take aim and fire at the looters. At least the quake has put paid to the boy racers, and you'll be pleased to know that the prostitutes have moved from Manchester Street to Ferry Road – as if anyone's got the time, the money, or the hygiene for that matter, for sex.

Company

Mind you, one of the gang here who is pushing sixty is in thrall over the quality of the army men and has said more than once, 'I may have a grey head but I'm not dead from the neck down.'

There was a quake in Wellington on Tuesday night, and I am imploring everyone there to get their survival kits together, especially matches, candles and water, and a little oil stove to boil water on. But the most important thing is company because the nights are long and lonely, and even if you have a rich interior life to fall back on you need people, otherwise the mind starts to unravel.

A drama-queen friend of mine rang up the other night to inform me she was phoning all her friends to tell them she felt very unsupported in that no one had offered to clean up her house. Not now you crazy bitch, it's not all about you, grow up infant, I thought, through gritted teeth. But I trotted out the platitudes. I was so angry afterwards I couldn't sleep, but I can't sleep anyway so what the heck – and anger's better than feeling sad.

My friend lives in a rich part of the city where there is no spontaneous community going on. Christchurch has always been a class-ridden town, a game of two halves, one half having huge tickets on itself about issues of breeding and entitlement, and the other half bashing whores and making racist attacks – fight stuff. But gosh, I've met some brilliant people in all of this. When it's all stripped back, when the mask falls down with the bricks, you find out what people are really like.

Cabin fever

MARCH 5 – The water's off again, coinciding with the beginnings of a dodgy tummy even though I've been careful to boil twice. Lighting the fire on which to put the preserving pan is now a no-no, with news of people being arrested for having al fresco fires, so the backyard gang were lucky to get away with it for as long as we did. I can understand that fire's a worry with water in short supply, but there are plenty of dried silt mounds from the bubbling crude lying round to expunge the flames.

Everyone was back in their hutches, as we call our tiny flats, and a feeling of normalcy was beginning to return to the place, but now most have vamooshed again, asking us to text them when we have water on. What would we do without our cell phones?

Early this morning I set off with loo paper, just in case I got caught out, and two large water containers. But first I needed petrol, and every damn station was cordoned off.

The tank was below empty and I found myself driving too far north, fearing I'd run out and have to ditch and hitch back into town, as I wriggled in my seat yelling, 'Where's a loo? Where's a bloody loo!' I found one, but by the time I got gas and arrived at the water station I must have looked more than a little wired and tired because the Red Cross guys walked across the road toward me, took the water cans out of my hands, filled them up, carried them back and put them in the boot for me. They were such gents I shed a tear as I took off.

Back at home there are rumblings in the ranks from those who decamped over how much rent we should have paid over the last days with no amenities working. People don't know if they have jobs any more and others are going to be flown all over the country to work from there.

Getting tradesmen through the cordon and linking up with the landlords – who have their own problems, having been evacuated from their Redcliffs' house – is a bureaucratic nightmare. Someone has to be here all the time to liaise as you never know when the required overworked official or tradesman etc will pass your way again. Ah well, the siege is young so we'd better get used to it.

I was talking to the Garage People this morning and asked the whereabouts of one of their constant hangers-on. Rodney told me he'd been taken off by the police after a hard night on the turps. I'm very pleased because he was, as Rodney described it, 'trying to staunch the street'.

I asked Rodney, a gentle soul, how he lost his front teeth and he told me he's a bad epileptic, had a fall a couple of years back, and came to *sans* fangs. He hadn't had a fit for a good six years and then two nights ago had a full on, grand mal seizure. 'The firemen from down the road sorted me out. They were really great. It must have been the quakes that set if off, eh?'

He's lost his flat, has no job and is living with Simon in a garage, but they cheerfully rise each morning and drive off to help someone else worse off (actually probably not) than them. Their landlord told me what honeys they are and that the fire station guys have adopted them.

The young guy who lives in the flat behind theirs is in construction, working in Linwood, and comes home at night beat from telling residents their homes are a write-off. 'Ninety percent of them take it really well but the others can't handle it,' he says, looking as shot as a messenger.

Yesterday I called in at the car yard to see the dealer who sold me the Suzuki Swift and tell him I might need a replacement, only to hear there aren't any left of the particular batch he'd sold me. Surprise, surprise, the only ones they had would be three grand more. Here we go.

Friends who want to visit don't get it that they can't come into the cordon. Even my brother with his dog collar and passport has no access because he's not on the list of residents with the right sticker and doesn't have a bill with an acceptable address – and he lives just down the road. To get our heads around the cabin fever we pretend that we are a very, very special branch of quakers who have to be minded by the armed forces. The big news is that the cordon may be reduced in a matter of days, which will be grand. If it doesn't happen, perhaps those within the cordon can form our own army, get out our sewing machines, knock up 'cordonite' uniforms and try and rush the curfew line.

Last night I heard what sounded like high-pitched castrati singing far off to the north of the city. It came again at dawn. The landlady who is camping in Woolston heard it too.

Italianate gestures

MARCH 7 – Two days ago I managed to get out to the parallel unspoiled universe that is Merivale to wash myself and some clothes before returning to the land where nothing works.

Saturday night around seven we were visited by the nastiest aftershock since the big Tuesday, which had me tearing the cap off a wine bottle to calm the shattered nerves. Made mental note to self – must remember to get a plumber in to install a new tap called sauvignon blanc next to the hot and cold.

The cordon has been shifted from Fitzgerald Avenue, but the Red Zone where civilians dare not enter stops at the Garage People's house. I went down there this morning to see that Simon and Rodney have got the Berlin Wall going on right in front of their noses. I can see Simon trying to work out if that's a good thing or a bad thing, while two army boys from the Hutt who flew down yesterday for a week's slog tell us they are working twelve hours on, twenty-four hours off. Call me sentimental but it's nice to have a bit of Wellington here.

The Garage guys went out and got some wood, turned their beds into bunks, and so have much more room in their gaff. There's an old sound system there and a whole swag of LPs so I must remember to ask if they have 'West of the Wall', the 1962 ditty about the Berlin Wall, so we can play it at two p.m. when the cordon's officially lifted.

Yesterday, pre army presence, Simon said he was going to celebrate the cordon coming down by getting in a 'dirty girl' before their female flatmate returns. (Clearly she holds the conscience of the house.) 'And the price is going to be negotiable,' Simon added.

I nearly died laughing. As I have mentioned, the prostitutes are down Ferry Road, and now in Deans Avenue too, Simon informs me. That's right next to Hagley Park and dangerously close to the gentrified suburb of Merivale. What Dionysian acts of trauma are being committed in the Wordsworthian daffodil beds one wonders?

Most streets have been cleared of the liquefaction and there are great piles of bricks stacked up. You see lines of people tossing the bricks one to the other to make light of the work. A volunteer coastguard accompanying residents back into our stretch of road says there are about thirty people living here now. No one is allowed in an area three blocks around the Grand Chancellor, and he was threatened with a thirty-day lock-up if he ventured into the wider Red Zone.

While we are talking, a resident from a red-stickered house

has an altercation with some builders. He walks back on to his property and shouts abuse at them. I have noticed that everyone has become more expressive, more Italianate in their gestures, with emotions running high. The coastguard, who is – correction, *was* – a property valuer before the quake, thinks the world as we know it will be radically different for the next ten years. 'A lot of people will have to dig deep inside themselves to find the so-called Canterbury spirit,' he says with a bitter grin.

Not many people have returned to our street, and rumour has it that the houses on the opposite side to mine will nearly all be demolished. It's cold and raining today and the coastguard tells me to go inside and watch the TV. 'I can't,' I say, and find myself brazenly asking him if he could take a look to make sure it's a goner. He does and pronounces it 'munted'. The word is used so much down here to sum up the devastation. *The Press* should print 'MUNTED' on the front page, like they did with the 'THANK YOU' in Saturday's paper to the very amazing people from all over the world who came to help us.

One fervently hopes that the rebuild of the city will be enlightened, and structured around walking and biking, with limited roads for buses and service vehicles. Yesterday a passenger car door swung open and I swerved into a cordoned area, the front wheel of my bike becoming lodged in a fissure. There was a colourful Italianate exchange of insults between driver and cyclist and I now have yet another bruise to add to the collection.

Italianate gestures

I am living about eight doors down from the Berlin Wall, but at least this dirty, as in unwashed, girl has close-by protection from the army. I'm going to make a sign saying, 'Hugs not thugs' and put it up outside the front gate.

Barney Rubble

MARCH 8 – I am standing at the part of the Red Zone that intersects Kilmore and Barbadoes Streets, watching two bulldozers tear down what was left of our groovy neighbourhood. All my quake mates are assembled, the plastic chairs are out in lines, and we watch as the two drivers manipulate their machines with Barney Rubble and Fred Flintstone synchronicity.

Piko Wholefoods, the beautiful brick organic food centre that magnificently withstood September 4, took a terrible pasting on February 22 and it is no surprise to us that the old beauty has to come down. Set up in 1979, Piko was responsible for the burgeoning of other like-minded – or spirited, I should say – shops: the Herbal Dispensary, the Retropolitan clothing store, an organic spa, a picture framer, and the cupcake shop that had only just moved into its brick building, after moving out of its previous premises after the last earthquake.

There's a whole swirl of officials mucking in on the other side of the fence – police, army, fire guys from Melbourne, demolition people, even Chinese rescue workers – all involved in the 'deconstruction', a word normally associated with artistic processes. Staff from the Herbal Dispensary turn up and beg the police to let them run across to their premises and retrieve patient files, only to be told, as the T. Rex machines carry on their attack, that they have to go across to Durham Street and get permission.

When the Herbal Dispensary sign is plucked from the roof, the female staff set up a wail for it not to be thrown on the rubbish; a Melbourne fire worker approaches the fence to tell them all is well, it has been kept aside. One of the herbal ladies puckers her lips through the fence and the Aussie fire guy obliges by meeting his smackers with hers.

The picture framer arrives, accompanied by a female companion carrying two roses to place outside his destroyed premises, but they are also not allowed in. The picture framer was uninsured – all his money was bound up in stock – but oh boy, is he lucky to be alive. I was sitting in the Herb Centre Café opposite his building when it fell to the ground, and I was convinced he must have been a No Way José. He's had an offer for work in Adelaide for three weeks, but after that who knows.

Vincent, the artist and neighbour our camp has befriended, has a fondness for found objects. He observes the wreckage, wishing he could forage for surfaces he could paint in order to create something out of the ruin. A couple of taxis of

Somali men turn up with armloads of home-made, plastic-wrapped meals and bottled drinks to pass through the gate to the workers. A man travelling with them says they have five hundred meals to deliver, are anxious to show that they are part of the community, and want to help in any way they can.

It seems hard to believe it is nearly two weeks since the terror that went on behind that cordon erupted. The days are meaningless, bleeding together, and the nights are to be dreaded, with dreams of a burning city and no decent sleep.

This morning the water returned – and high-pressure stuff too. Fingers crossed it will stay. However, I still put buckets and saucepans outside to catch the rain and replenish the survival kit, and always leave a pack by the door when it gets dark, to get out fast.

I went to a community barbecue on Sunday peopled by the weird and wonderful: a mature-aged cross-dresser, another man talking to himself and darting eyes right and left, wearing boots without a speck of mud, an unusual sight in a town that is just beginning to stop resembling the mud in Deadwood. You wonder: did these people go mad before the quake or were they always like this?

Men you knew who were smooth-faced now sport quake beards, and women are developing Brooke Shields eyebrows. We all apologise to each other for conversations where we lose our concentration, can't find the right word, stare off, and laugh at a brain that's not back in its box yet. The quakes have left us full of twitch and jump as we stare through the wire into the forbidden city.

The postman cometh

MARCH 9 – Unbelievable! Yesterday morning there was a loud knock at the door – a courier with a package from Sky TV. There have been no paper and no mail for two weeks, but here was the courier arriving, bearing a promotional gift. Not quite what I had hoped for but at least some pigeon mail is getting through.

When the power went off again in the middle of the night, I lay awake in the shakes thinking about having to choose between water or power – a debate I discussed with Dave, my aged parents' old neighbour when I paid him a visit up in Mt Pleasant. He knew it was me by the loud knock, which he takes as my implication he's deaf, and because every time I visit him I never fail to catch him on the throne.

'So you've got the water on then,' I shouted to him from outside.

Dave thinks my preference for water over power is typical of women and that men want the power. A little early in the morning for the battle of the sexes, I tell him, but it was great to see him in such shape. He'd only just got the water on but had no power; four houses had already been demolished in his immediate area and the keen photographer in him is going nuts over missed opportunities to be blazing away. He hands me the binoculars to look down the hill toward what is left of the city, and the drunken angle of the Grand Chancellor hotel. The once familiar arrangement of skyscrapers now looks like the CBD has been in a fight and had most of its teeth knocked out.

Dave is looking after my parents' old house, where I resided for more than two years until just after the first quake, and we go over to water the plants. I know it's silly but I am proud to see that this house – so vilified by two real estate agencies that failed to flog it off for us before a third sold it – is standing strong, completely unscarred. Everyone is curious to find out the condition of former houses they've lived in and I am relieved to see with my own eyes that our family didn't sell the new owners a dud.

I have to get to Paddy, my computer guy, who lives in a new subdivision in Ferrymead where the roads hiccup with bumps so much it's like having a workout for the hips as I swing the steering wheel madly like a hoon, trying to avoid the holes.

Problem solved, and as I'm over that way I take the opportunity to shoot through to Lyttelton to Leslie's Book Shop to pick up my weekly order of magazines. The father and son who run the shop have a lovely patter and always ring if there is any hold-up. Even though I know from reports it's unlikely they are up and running, old habits die hard.

I take a deep breath and drive into the tunnel, which is flanked at the Heathcote end by two-deep, six-long high-stacked containers. Imagine that lot falling on you, I awfulise as I plunge into the tunnel in a line of slow-moving cars, trying to contain the claustrophobia.

The two main streets of Lyttelton closest to the port are a sad sight, brick hotels and buildings in shocking states of collapse. I can't get into the bookshop as the road is closed and I realise this weekly journey is another routine taken out of a life now radically altered.

Driving back into the city, every church left standing that I pass is conducting a funeral. You wonder about the crowds clustered out on the street and then it hits you. The dead are being sent on their way and I don't like to think about any of it.

Back at Kilmore Street, the tear-down continues at the intersection, but at least the bottom floor of Piko Wholefoods and its logo still stand. The owners had not been notified of the deconstruction, and when they received a text from a neighbouring business they managed to get a stay of execution.

I see a postie disappearing down my street. I run out to the letterbox but amazingly it is empty. Maybe tomorrow…

Speaking in tongues

MARCH 10 – Yesterday another uniform appeared in the street so I approached the lady with the blue bib that said 'chaplain' and asked her where she was from. She said her name was Judy and that she was a Pentecostal Christian from Sydney, over here to stand alongside of us in our time of need. Judy had been doing the same thing with the floods back home. There had been five hundred of her ilk door-knocking there, so when her mob found out there were only two Kiwi Pentecostals on the ground here five of them got on a plane to lend a hand.

I looked at her hands to see if she was giving out anything such as a brochure, water, a dry biscuit perhaps, but no, it was just her tongue, which, if I remember rightly, Pentecostals speak in.

I said, 'We are expecting Sean Penn or Angelina and Brad to arrive any minute' and she said, 'Well, people often tell me that I look like Sigourney Weaver – will that do?'

I thought, you're not a bad for a holy roller, so I told her I could see the resemblance and asked her, from the locals she'd been talking to, what sort of shape she thought we were in.

'Everyone's very worried there'll be another one and wanting to leave town on March 20,' she said.

Yup, that's right. I bought into Ken Ring's predictions too, but now I think Old Bucky, as I call the earthquake, has had his fun with Canterbury. Humans have a complete cell change every seven years and Earth is doing the same, so we just have to ride it out and try and stay in the saddle 'til he stops kicking.

Campfires are awash with conspiracy theories that the presence of a bunch of international urologists in the city and a frigate in Lyttelton on the day of the shake were not just a coincidence: the government knew something was going to happen, hence its incredibly swift response.

I almost expected to see some reference to these viral myths on the Tui billboard on my way out to Sumner, when I had to wait at makeshift lights underneath the long stretch of road in Redcliffs where the cliff has eroded so badly. The green light couldn't come fast enough as I worked out that if a half-decent twitch happened to hit I'd be out the car door and into the sea – and back again, I supposed, with a tsunami.

The brain is constantly working out exit strategies, the antennae checking out how long it will take to bike under a verandah that might collapse, the eyes looking down at the road to avoid cracks and bumps, always on hyper alert.

The power had been off again for a couple of days at Kilmore Street and I was beginning to resemble 'Dan, Dan, dirty old man, washed his face with a frying pan, combed his hair with the leg of a chair', as my grandfather used to recite, so when a night in Sumner was offered I took it.

I had seen my friend only once since the quake, when we raced my cat to the vet, and we sat on her deck looking out to the beautiful sea talking as fast as racing commentators, trying to download all our experiences and information as quickly as we could. She inquired after Benecio, the Maine Coon, and I was happy to inform her the vet had just phoned to say he had been successfully nuked for his hyperthyroid complaint, and now a husband-and-wife team, big in knees and eyes, will, one working at the top end and one at the bottom, operate on his quake-related affliction. By the time I spring him from that cattery he's going to be The Six Million Dollar Cat.

Life in Eastern Europe

MARCH 11 – The mail arrived for the first time yesterday – three bills and a handwritten, unsigned letter from a religious nutter telling me that Armageddon is nigh and to stop my cynical ways. How typical, I thought, screwing it up and throwing it across the room, wondering where my three copies of the *Listener* had got to.

With the power the way it is, filing copy is proving frustrating and my settings are dodgy. I limp my laptop back to Paddy, my computer guy, and he lets me power it up. As I do so I hear him on the phone to computer idiots like myself, who have rung in to say that since he fixed their PC their printer won't go. Turns out they had put in a new cartridge, which caused the problem. 'I get a lot of people ringing up saying pathetic stuff like, "Since you fixed my PC I can't hang my washing out,"' Paddy says. He lets me stay until the computer's charged and I am grateful: he is a calm, funny bloke and it feels normal here in Ferrymead.

During the daytime the three other people left in our two households go to work, leaving me alone in the Quiet Earth zone. As is my routine, I go out to the gate every half-hour for a nosey, and to see if I can bail up an Orion worker and get him to put the power back on. The street lamps go, so why not our houses? It doesn't make any sense, so all you can do is phone daily and hope they'll turn up some time. I imagine this must be what it's like living in an Eastern European country.

So there I was at the end of the drive and this really – I mean totally – wild-eyed low-life guy skids to a halt on his bike and asks me how to get into the city. Dodgy and thick I instantly judge him, as I slowly explain that the cordon where he has just come from is the barrier to the Red Zone, which civilians are not allowed to enter.

'What's a civilian?' he asks, looking at my cell phone and keys.

'An ordinary person like you and me,' I tell him.

He asks if I have a phone inside the house.

No way is he getting his cotton-picking hands on my cell phone and absolutely no way is he coming in my flat, so I say sorry, I don't have any money left on the cell and no landline, hoping like hell that the cell doesn't ring while we're speaking.

'I have to go to court today,' he says, and I think, I bet you do mate, I bet you do.

'There won't be any court at the moment, don't worry about it,' I tell him and find myself talking about 'my husband in the backyard'. He finally bikes off and I think, hell, do I have to organise a boyfriend in the middle of all this for some protection?

I know it's silly but ever since the big one struck I have been wearing a whistle around my neck on some rope so rescuers can hear me if I get buried in rubble. Get a grip, girl – but hey, better to look silly than be sorry.

A friend came over last night and stayed, and we got quite snippy with each other and had cross words, with me yelling at her, 'Don't tell me what to do in my own house!' But this morning, after she and I slept in the lounge together, we are grudge-free and hugging each other, she is thanking me for having her to stay, and we are laughing as I imitate her snores. It's like being back at boarding school.

Those in our two houses who have gone elsewhere have left me their keys. I clang around the place like a jailer as friends of theirs arrive to get out stuff they have stored in their houses. Lug, lug, shift, drift – it's all so aimless.

I know a really great couple who live in Richmond, where I drift off to with my endless computer problems, and they're always loading me up with fruit and vegetables. To my stunned incredulity, Frances announced to me yesterday that she was off out to get her legs waxed and I thought where – Paris? Her husband pretends to be mad that his daughters, who have come home to park up after problems with their flats, are using his razor to shave their legs. It's hard for us girls trying to keep ourselves nice.

Jerk patrol

MARCH 12 – What joy it is to hear the hot breath of the kettle boiling in the kitchen now that I have the power back on.

I got home yesterday to find the lounge light glowing. This was after a trying altercation with a member of the jerk patrol, as I call some of the constabulary with a deficit of common sense who are controlling our lives. A simple drive home along Fitzgerald Avenue to Kilmore Street could not happen because there was a massive tear-down of buildings at that corner, so traffic was being rerouted down Armagh Street. It hadn't occurred to whoever thought up that bright idea that Armagh Street ceases to be a conduit of civilian traffic when it meets Barbadoes Street.

I saw a car park at the side of the road, threw my car into it and, with my laptop bag strapped across my chest, a pack on my back and holding another bag, I walked up to a cop and told him I was trying to get home to Kilmore Street. The only way that was going to happen was for me to walk along the inside border of the Red Zone, I said. 'How do I know you live in Kilmore Street?' he said, asking for proof.

So we're back to that again, I thought, explaining to him that the cordon had been lifted three days ago, I no longer lived in the forbidden zone, and so there was no further need to carry that kind of ID. I showed him my passport but he shook his head, wanting a bill or a letter with my address on it, so I sat down in the gutter and unpacked everything, going through it all again and again, hoping to find the bill I had been carrying around in the old days, but alas I must have dispensed with it. Because you have to carry a lot with you – cell phone, keys, passport, survival kit, water, laptop, etc etc etc – obsessive compulsive disorder descends as you continually check you have all the vitals.

The cop was observing my frustration and I said to him, 'Am I to live in this gutter then?' noting I had resorted to a biblical speech pattern. After a very, very long time he caved in and told me I could scoot home, but if anyone asked what I was doing in the Red Zone I was not to implicate him.

The big news on the street this morning is the tear down of Simon and Rodney's old house across the road. A grader driver who is touring the South Island is watching the demolition approvingly. Rodney says, 'There's Simon's old bed' as the bulldozer's claw delicately hoists the bed in the air, before dropping it in the rubble.

It is, or was, a two-storey, eight-bedroom concrete building and the demolition is done and dusted in under an hour. The operator gets out of the cab with Olympian calm, locks the door, and I give him a round of applause as Rodney wonders if there are going to be celebrity grader drivers.

The owner of the house was on the street and beside herself this morning; Rodney had to give her a big hug and apply soothing words. She has properties on the next street that are in trouble too so she has a lot on her plate. Rodney hopes their garden out the back is still intact because he's got swede, beans and spinach in there and it would be such a waste.

The visiting bulldozer operator is trying to get work here and be part of the clean-up but he can't get accommodation for a hundred miles. My aunt and uncle have the same problem as their house waits to be fixed up.

Simon asks me if I want to go for a jaunt to Rangiora to visit his flatmate, but I want to get to Hornby and check out Benecio. I tell Simon that when my Maine Coon is back on his feet he's coming for his four budgies – L2, the Minister of Finance, Jumbo Jan and Trevor, the homosexual. Why homosexual you may ask? Because Trevor has his way with Jumbo Jan and then pashes up the Minister of Finance, Simon explains.

Pomeroy's, the pub on the corner, was supposed to open tomorrow but it won't happen 'til early next week and the publican has asked if my brother can bless it before the first pour, which he is only too happy to do. Having the hostelry up and running will be a huge step toward civilisation. As Gary, a friend of mine puts it, 'It'll just be great to be able to go there with your mates and swap quake stories and say, "You think your toilet's bad. Listen to this…"' What sweet banality that will be.

The new normal

MARCH 14 – I had just settled down on the couch with a rug to watch *Campbell Live* on Friday night when breaking news brought harrowing pictures of the devastation going down in Japan.

Poor Japan. Only a week ago I had received an email from my first ever boyfriend, who lives there half the year, to ask if I were still in the land of the living in Christchurch. Now I jump on the computer to ask the same question, quickly receiving an email back to say that all are unhurt: at the time of the earthquake he just happened to be visiting Osaka, 900 kilometres away from the worst hit city, Sendai, where he has a house.

Last I heard from him he was trying to see if the trains were running so he could check out whether his house had survived, and I thought, good luck with that. He finished off his missive with the line: 'It seems we're competing, the gods are upset.'

All thoughts of a good night's sleep and turning in early were shot after observing that carnage, so when a couple of the Garage People hammered on my door to invite me down to their place I accepted with alacrity. There was the usual odd collection milling around at the Berlin Wall. Kirsty is only nineteen and was suffering separation anxiety because the army lad she had been chatting with all day had just gone off his shift. Now she was checking out the new shift, admiring their 'cute butts'.

'Oh, to be nineteen again,' Simon said.

The radio was on full volume and belting out the Eagles when the music broke for more bad news of Japan and we all howled in unison for it to shut up. Simon took to his bunk, where he sleeps next to a pink butterfly net and a large flaccid pink panther dangling sadly from the roof.

'Take me now God! Take me to the house of the dirty girls! I'm ready Lord,' he wailed.

Honestly, he is the dizzy limit. One of the Garage People had gone away to Rangiora for a few days to stay with her daughter but didn't feel right out there. She is suffering from survivor guilt as she was working in the hotel next to the Grand Chancellor and didn't have time to check all the rooms on her floor. She is traumatised, re-running in her head the long climb down the hotel stairs and the shattering walk home, and is going to a counsellor tomorrow.

A motorbike has come to a halt outside the Deaf Society building on Armagh Street and is resting next to where the army lads congregate. A couple of days ago the intoxicated owner of said motorbike had sped along Kilmore Street attempting to break the cordon and had come a cropper on the wire. The army boys thought it was a huge joke and sent him limping on his unmerry way.

On Sunday Millie and I start to unscramble our garage, where we camped out in that first week. There are some rotten fruit and vegetables; we clean it up and reclaim all our stuff, making it shipshape and Bristol fashion as Miriam is returning soon and would be disgusted at our reckless abandonment of the camp. But we don't get rid of the wood we dragged in to keep it dry, and also leave a few necessities and bare bones in case Old Bucky returns for some more of his knee-jerk reactions.

On Saturday the roads were congested but by Sunday you can hear a pin drop out there. I bike along the deserted streets with ease on a grey day where no birds sing. My nephew phones to say he's gone back to work at the university campus, where some of the lectures are taking place in large tents. His boss gathered staff together and opened his speech with the new expression now heard in Devastation City: 'Welcome to the new normal.'

Mars might be nice

MARCH 15 – In the middle of the night it occurs to me that in light of the mega horror going down in Japan, this post-quake reportage of my petty problems and peregrinations is very small beer indeed. Observing the photographs and TV footage of Japan's plight from down here at the fag end of the world makes us reflect that we got off lightly, as the magnitude is updated to a whopping nine and we hear how the Earth was actually knocked off its axis.

Talk about special effects – even Mr Spielberg and Weta Workshop combined couldn't recreate such lurid natural disasters. At least we know a year out who will win the next Oscar for special effects – God.

'What's happening to the world?' everyone asks, shaking their heads and wondering what part of the Pacific Rim Old Bucky will strike at next.

I read my brother's past Sunday sermon about the quake, which he hands to me for perusal over a sundowner partaken in his office, the only building he has left in its entirety in his world. In the sermon he reminds his flock how the bible specifically warns against taking heed of diviners and soothsayers who use illegitimate means to predict a fate, which is not ours to know. It is easy to give into despair and imagine the world coming to an end, but we must keep a cool head, remembering the good that has come out of the quake – the kindness of strangers, the sharing of a universal experience, and the real sense of a community pulling together.

'Dad would have liked that one,' I tell him.

His son arrives and tells of an almighty pong that now emanates from the battered suburbs of Opawa and St Martins, how he sniffs the air before getting on his bike to judge the prevailing wind and chooses a route that does not offend the olfactory senses.

As I drive out to Marshlands to refuel I am in awe of the massive effort that has been made to sort out the buckle and crack, the crazy paving of the roads, smoothing and sealing so now the awful dust has subsided and most people have dispensed with their face masks.

I pull into a large roadside vegetable produce place that has a separate little hut selling real fruit ice cream and coffee. Two other vendors are now dotted around the car park: a designer sausage outfit and the German bakery that used to reside in the Arts Centre. As the baker mans his stall he explains that his core business was supplying bread to the hotels in the CBD. How swiftly he has got with the programme of the new reality and is turning a diminished dime, but at least a dime, in a far-off location. The owner of the vegetable store has given him the first month rent-free and then they'll negotiate. As Mr Darwin said – adapt and change or get left behind.

I visit friends in a well-heeled suburb that experienced significantly bad liquefaction. Their mounds of dirt have been taken away but the weekend after the quake, when everyone was shovelling like mad, a couple of cars came barrelling along the road, whipping up the dust. Harry motioned with his hand for them to slow down, eliciting a foul-mouthed verbal attack from the occupants of the car, a bunch of skinheads who threatened him with a 'We know where you live.'

'I mean, what were they doing here?' Harry says, admitting that if the driver had got out of the car and had a go he would cheerfully have beaten him with his shovel, reckoning the rest of the street, full of anaesthetists and doctors, would have joined in.

Tribal lines have been blurred. People are out of their boxes as passers-by in cars, holding cameras in a Hail Mary salute, film the rubble of their lives. The Earth has growled and shaken not quite so much in the last couple of days, delivering a false sense of security: we know there is more energy to be released, hopefully in dollops we can cope with.

I wonder whatever happened to the idea of building on Mars. Reinventing myself as another girl on another planet seems quite a good option about now, until I remember they don't have the power and water on either.

Rough trade

MARCH 16 – The gridlock of traffic on the avenues had prevented me from getting out to the veterinarian clinic to visit Benecio, the beloved feline, until Monday. Surgery to his knee and eye had been delayed, and he was doped up on morphine, managing to emit only the faintest of purrs.

I was vexed to discover that after his op Benecio will need caging to restrict movement so the intricate knee surgery has a chance to heal. 'How long does he have to be caged for?' I ask, to which the nurse replies, 'Some weeks' and offers to lend me a cage slightly bigger than the one I transported him in.

Oh dear, what a life for the Maine Coon. Maybe Siegfried and Roy could lend us one of their tiger cages for the incarceration period.

Getting a replacement television took about five hours in ridiculous traffic and when I got to Cash Converters in Papanui they'd sold their last one. I drove, hot and bothering in the heat, with my truck-driver's arm resting on the open window, slowly in the opposite direction to the soulless Tower Junction Megacentre. There I found a helpful salesman who did me an EQC deal, so this afternoon I'll be back in the land of Sky TV, but I dread the sight of quake porn writ large.

I have had another email from my friend in Japan, describing the natural (quake and tsunami) and unnatural (nuclear) disasters as 'cataclysmic – I dare not say apocalyptic'.

When it's dark I go out to Ferry Road to buy fish and chips and notice two strangely configured prostitutes plying for trade on the side of the road. One is fat and old and has just been dropped off from an assignation, while the other on the opposite side of the street is young and must be at least seven months pregnant. Do people actually pay for this?

The next morning I rise early and drive out to Upper Riccarton to get my shopping done at a supermarket that opens at six a.m. On the way home in the crepuscular dawn I make out some very tidy-looking whores pacing the corner of Bealey Avenue and Manchester Street. I suppose this must be the top end of the curb-crawling trade, where the girls make an effort with their appearance, as opposed to the rough gravel paths of Ferry Road and the skanks on offer there.

Now the liquefaction mounds have been dealt to, the boy racers have come back into play and spend the early hours knocking over witch's hats that cordon and map the road for bumps. No paper delivery yet and with the dairy over the road out of action it's a good stretch of the legs to get the printed skinny on the Forbidden City. The colony of aging transvestites who used to hang out and sit on chairs outside Haast Place to watch the dusty inching of traffic along Stanmore Road seems to have disappeared back inside.

Last night a sign was pinned to a Fitzgerald Avenue tree announcing that our local Beat Street Café was back in business and to enter it along Armagh Street. The other street the corner café breasts is Barbadoes in the Red Zone.

It is wonderful to know there is real coffee, just like a bought one, around the corner and this morning I paced over, ordered, and took a seat in Checkpoint Charlie. A clutch of army, police and navy personnel milled around outside taking photos of each other. Beat Street has filled some biggish orders from Fulton and Hogan workers, but apart from me none of the locals left in the area have trickled back, so the manager will give it a couple of days and see how it goes.

On the way home I stop and chat to a neon-jacketed worker astride a canvassed area about two containers long, under which major work is being done on damage to the electricity cable. Our power is currently coming from a massive generator dumped at the end of Kilmore Street in the Commerce Club's car park. It makes quite a hum but has done us proud for the last few days. I ask him how long until we're hooked up to the national grid and he says a couple of days max. So we will have power to the people in a town made ghostly – thanks mostly to the man in the moon.

Robin comes over for the last time to borrow the keys to get his belongings out of Marion's shed. He's leaving tomorrow for Wellington for good, never coming back, but can't get his bond back unless his flat is cleaned out. With all side walls having fallen down, everything inside a mess of glass and debris, and the place red-stickered, that is a ridiculous ask, especially as neither the property manager nor the out-of-town landlord have inspected it yet. I wish him the best of luck for the future and watch yet another drive off dragging a trailer load.

Friends and neighbours

MARCH 17 – Before the last quake, I used to joke to a friend that the large, white, two-storey house a few doors down, which had its curtains drawn permanently day and night and never showed a flicker of electric light, housed the Lost Tribe of Albinos. That fabrication couldn't have been further from the truth as I witnessed the exodus of tenants from the yellow-stickered house and noted they were all of Asian descent.

The impressive two-storey weatherboard further down on the opposite side of the road I never paid any heed to either, until these past weeks when I got chatting with Andrew, who, when we were without water, kindly let me have access to an artesian spring he had veined into in his backyard. Andrew resides in one of the many rooms in the boarding house rented by older Pakeha men who, from all accounts, have been knocking round the inner city most of their adult lives. Politeness forbids me from asking if they had jobs before the quake, but it is interesting to note how many of the middle-aged men in this street hail from a farming background.

I take heart from this at night when I listen to the radio and learn the true meaning of the expression 'too much information' as a myriad of possible reasons are trotted out for the chaos in which we currently find the planet – for example, the Earth is slipping off its magnetic field; the sun is spotting solar flares; the Hadron Collider, in its quest for dark matter, has unleashed unimaginable power.

Callers phone into talkback to say get out of the city, buy some land and start alternative living, which is where the farming chaps come in as I imagine all of us in the street uprooting and going to build again upcountry in a brave new survivor world. And then that good old stick dawn finally arrives to chase the tiny demons away.

No radio station can get off-topic as quakes, tsunamis and nuclear meltdowns nexus into each other and I find myself longing for the good old days when life was so dull that the scandal of Tuku Morgan's underpants and Rodney Hide's spear tackle on *Dancing with the Stars* dominated the news for weeks.

My new replacement television is not a going concern yet. A technician came yesterday and set it up, only to find that the Sky dish, in unison with the planet, has been knocked off its axis. Now I wait for the Sky man to cometh.

The only movie theatre in town is way out in Hornby so I rely on dreams for my visuals, the good news being that my last recurring quake nightmare featured the new character of a turbaned man sitting cross-legged on a hovering magic carpet.

Even though I have water now and don't need access to Andrew's house, I make a point of getting off my bike whenever he yells out, 'How ya goin'?' That once easy, meaningless greeting now means so much more as we who are not strangers or friends either make sure to give each other a chunk of our time, let each other say their piece. Small polite chats demonstrate you are of honest intent and have a sincerity of purpose, because it's so much wiser and easier to help someone than hurt them, now we're getting to the shabby part of this experience.

By this time you've sorted out the wrong 'uns, the flakes and the non-performers, and it's every man and woman for themselves: if it's not a two-way street of mutual help or a contra deal, people are dropping the users over the side. Each of us has had plenty of time to sort out the bare necessities and become self-reliant in order to be a functioning, non-draining unit, thus contributing to getting the city back on its feet. There are no haves and have nots, just people who, if they are good to you, you are good back to.

Before nightfall I like to take a stroll down to what was the lovely box seat of the Avon Loop. The dreamy, vigilantly preserved, heritage riverside houses that the local residents fought so hard to keep away from the itchy hands of developers are all on wonky angles, their foundations sunk well into the ground, the road a cracked-up mess. Those living near the river have been badly affected, but it is hard to keep away from the loveliness and calm of the Avon as it is so much part and parcel of this city. Perhaps in keeping with the Anglophile leanings of Christchurch, the river should be turned into a giant *Wind in the Willows* theme park. The beauty of that notion is that we already have the main characters – Ratty, Mole, Toad, Badger, the washerwoman, and the weasels, stoats and ferrets – firmly in place.

Crescendos of collapse

MARCH 18 – The vet has just phoned to inform me that Benecio has come through his operation magnificently. His eye has been successfully fixed but he no longer has a knee ligament: it's just bone on bone. 'Couldn't I have given him one of my ligaments?' I ask her, explaining that a human to cat transfer would be the ultimate gift. I'm sure if Dr Christiaan Barnard were alive he would have had a crack at it.

Benecio has to stay in for a further week so they can keep him on pain relief. Although I miss him something shocking, it's best he's out of harm's way I think, as I hear the landlord up on the roof biffing down more bricks from the wreckage of three chimneys and knocking down damaged concrete fences.

The Red Zone continues to emit a cacophony of unusual noises one can't quite identify – high-pitched drills, flurries of sirens, crescendos of collapse – as everything that can be torn down is torn down. Our dairy was bulldozed yesterday and masks were slapped on again as there is a lot of asbestos flying around. The army boys took it in turns to lift a 1.5-kilogram weight, bending toward the bulldozer as it went about its destructive business, as if they were paying homage to the great machine.

Whenever you go past a park you see mothers sitting quietly under a tree with their young, while the gym-deprived seem to be conducting workouts in any green space they can find.

The vet rings me back in the hope I might have kept a backlog of newspapers she can mine for her kid's project on the quake. Alas, I have chucked most out and tell her to go online and use printouts: surely that would do, and any teacher would understand everyone is stretched. She has three children all attending schools that share facilities for half a day each. The children come home drowning under a sea of homework she has to supervise.

The death notices in the paper spill out to over two pages, many of them starting with the all too familiar words 'Taken tragically by the earthquake of February 22'. Shiny black hearses slink through dusty gravel roads carrying coffins to the few-and-far-between churches still standing, and you hope the dead are given a proper send-off, that's it's not too rushed, as funeral parlors are crisply processing three a day.

Millie comes over with Toby in a cat box to take to her vet as he has been in a terrible fight, and, without Benecio as backup, has incurred nasty wounds that if left unattended over the long weekend will probably turn septic. We pile him into the courtesy car and take off, returning with antibiotics for the Tobster and the discovery that the power has gone out again. We traipse down to the generator, where a Corporal Jones type is happy to inform us that they're on top of the situation, they're changing a filter and it'll be back on in a jiffy.

'Very good, carry on the good work,' I say in Captain Mannering style.

Down at the Armagh Street end of Checkpoint Charlie, the Beat Street café is doing a roaring trade and I'm so pleased for them. The manager proudly tells me it has become the army's intersection of choice. They and the police order their flat whites while the local clientele, in their uniform of dreadlocks, studs, and the mandatory one arm of tattoos for the ladies, try to accept the new presence of grunts and overlords.

The landlord, who lives in Redcliffs where the cliff came down, asks me if I'm going to come to Sumner tomorrow to see Prince William. What's Wills going to do there? Stand under the cliff? Or go look at Shag Pile, as Shag Rock is now called? No, I tell the landlord, I'm going to the memorial service tomorrow in the park, and if Mr Ring is right the ground will open up and we can all be tidily buried in a mass grave as Hayley Westenra sings her wee lungs out. Just kidding.

My magazine men are now up and running in the Lyttelton Health Centre building so I'm off over there to pick up nearly a month's worth of orders. I'll kill two birds with one stone as Archie, the fisherman, has just texted to say he's pulling the boat up at the jetty at five-thirty p.m. and there's red cod and flounder a-plenty. A really good day.

Goodbye to the republic

MARCH 19 – Normally I avoid crowds, anything that makes me feel like an ant, but I'm glad I rode down to Hagley Park to attend the Christchurch Memorial Service today. Over the past few weeks we have been too preoccupied to notice that autumn has come upon us. Today it felt like the middle of summer again as thick queues of subdued Cantabrians poured into the park to find a place to sit, watch, listen and give thanks.

This was an al fresco church service, not a concert, and the crowd had taken that on board. There were no hot-dog stands, no quake T-shirts and no face-painting booths, although there was a tent offering free massages, the Sallies were giving out free water, and those who have been consigned to portaloos marvelled at the high quality of the toilets.

A couple on motorised scooters had literally parked up their vehicles and brought along a small table to assemble their drinks. It had taken them forty minutes to get from Burnside and the gentleman of the party was slightly worried he might run out of battery juice for the journey home. Nothing had happened to their house or their family, and, suffering from a bad case of survivor guilt, they had desperately wanted to come to the service and pay their respects.

Four massive TV screens were hung around the park and when the silent footage screened of the never-before-seen devastation of what has become the Forbidden City, you couldn't hear a child wriggle or the proverbial pin drop. The only noise came from the film footage, with its wail of sirens, sound of helicopters sirens, and occasional chorus of birds.

The video, simply showing the street names then taking the viewer on an odyssey of pain and discovery to see buildings once so fond and familiar now disfigured and strange, was more affecting than the two minutes of silence the battered south has become used to. The crowd were as quiet as the grave as they stood and contemplated the dead.

I sat among a crowd of strangers who applauded equally John Key's and Phil Goff's speeches but the man of the moment was definitely Prince William. There is absolutely no chance of New Zealand becoming a republic now that the royal family has sent out the young prince, rather than the old jug-eared one, to commiserate with the colonies, to shake our hands while distributing his mother's common touch and his father's Windsor protocol.

Dave Dobbyn was the first and only contemporary musician in the service. After so many speeches that had to make mention of our brothers and sisters in Japan facing a worse fate than ours, it was a relief to hear him give thanks to all the brave rescue workers, police and firemen who came to help us in our hour of need. But when Hayley Westenra got up and sang 'Amazing Grace' it absolutely killed me. Her voice has matured so much. My god she held it, she really held it, managing to make that corny, overly sung hymn new again.

And Timua Brennan was so staunch, far better than any Kiri – where was Kiri in all of this? – as her voice shook the pillars of pink and white petunias, warbling across the huge crowd 'How Great Thou Art' so loud and true it would have stirred Sir Howard in his grave.

After the multicultural prayers that were so moving and simple, Hayley took to the stage again to give an impromptu rendition of 'Pokarekare Ana' as the slender prince, with his retinue of bodyguards and the PM and the GG trailing in his wake, reached out to the grieving families who had lost loved ones, then moved through the crowd shaking as many hands as he could.

What a day, what a ceremony, not an alcoholic drink in sight, not a heckle of bad behaviour that I could see, and the ground shaking only with the sound of song. Stick that in your pipe and smoke it, Ken Ring.

Bless this house

MARCH 21 – Tomorrow it will be a month since the quake and most of us want the Red Zone to be over and done with. But if you have lived in Christchurch all your life, grown up here, married, had your children here, and are now in the winter of your life, then you are in no hurry to see the hugely altered CBD.

My uncle, who is in his eighties, told me his approach to reacquainting himself with the muntage that is the interior of the city will be to see it a little at a time. He knows he may not be around for the rebuild so he doesn't have the purchase on the future that younger generations have.

On Friday night a miracle happened. Pomeroy's, our local pub, reopened and the publican did indeed ask my brother Hugh, the vicar, to bless the premises. Happy to oblige, Hugh slapped on his dog collar and said a prayer for Poms, 'our oasis of hospitality', giving particular thanks to the microbrewers of New Zealand, asking that the good Lord 'continues to endow with skill your servants Richard Emerson, Ralph Bungard, Luke Nicholas and all the local wonder-workers with hops'. It went down a treat.

This morning it felt like Christmas as Sean Plunket arrived with loo paper and a box of Roses Chocolates, followed by Gerry Morris, who had phoned to say he was passing through and was going to drop off some mouthwash, then turned up shortly afterwards with three bottles of plonk. Talk about spoilt, I felt like baby Jesus.

In town to host a lunch organised by the New Zealand Skeptics at Sign of the Kiwi, Sean asked if I wanted to tag along. You bet, so we piled into a car and drove up to the Port Hills, as close as possible to the epicentre of the earthquake that Ken Ring divined was to hit at midday.

Outside the hostelry a skeptic had slapped the following note to a pole: 'The vibrations caused by incautious movement, in conjunction with the position of the moon and a major accumulation of bovine excreta on the news media, may trigger the catastrophic collapse of the Port Hills at any time.' The author had signed himself Len Thing – qualified prognosticator and pontificator, tea leaves read, futures told, media interviews a specialty.

Vicky Hyde, chair of the Skeptics, and Mark Ottley, a clinical psychologist at St Georges Hospital who has been dealing at the sharp end of the suffering, administering to those with amputations and spinal damage, spoke with not inconsiderable vehemence about the damage Mr Moon has inflicted on vulnerable Cantabrians.

Bless this house

The owner of Sign of the Kiwi, enjoying the roaring trade the function had brought her, said how bad for business Mr Moon had been, with so many Christchurch residents fleeing the city. A call was made that Ring should give an apology to the people of Christchurch, and if the 'peddler of pseudo information', as Hyde described him, had walked into the room I fear he would not have made it out with breath in his body.

The MPs Nick Smith and Nicky Wagner were present and Skeptic Society members who are residents of Redcliffs related how ineffective Civil Defence had been in the suburbs. With Civil Defence points unmanned and unlocked, they have been left to develop their own grassroots information points as residents give up and leave town.

Twelve noon came and went as we sat in the rock restaurant and heard how Ring had downgraded his prediction to 'an extreme weather event worldwide'. Outside, the soft Irish rain that had started in the morning continued to gently fall, the hills that have grown a foot taller, stood their sturdy ground, and you could hear the birdies sing. Ring was wrong.

A bloody good cat

MARCH 28 – Benecio arrived home last Tuesday for the first time in over three weeks, and immediately started throwing his weight around. I had prepared for his incarceration by locking the cat door, after strict instructions from the vet to keep him inside and on the flat, with no jumping or leaping allowed. The legs of the bed had been unscrewed as I knew he would want to snuggle up, but there was no way I was going to saw the legs off the reproduction antique table made by my grandfather, the French polisher.

As soon as he got out of the cage Benecio was charging round the joint, jumping on chairs and ledges and ramming his head at the cat door trying to get out. After an hour of such shenanigans I heard a great clatter and turned to see him actually shouldering the cat door, breaking it down.

I consulted the pussy whisperer from next door as we sat outside with our cats, Benecio limping round the property sniffing and peeing up his songlines in the backyard until he calmed down. Prior to his operation he was such a handsome lad, but now there is a huge gouge over one eye and no eyebrow whiskers, and his left leg, shaved poodle-style, bears a nasty scar. Ah, but how sweet to have him home again. If I could lay my hands on a pram I'd wheel him round the neighbourhood to show him off, just like Rhett Butler with his beloved daughter Bonnie in *Gone With The Wind*.

Speaking of wildlife, the birds still behave oddly, ripping the air with loud harsh screeches. Gulls and huge terns hang out like gangsters slap bang in the middle of Kilmore Street and ducks quack piteously from the river. You also see rats running along fence lines, and enormous flies, as big as Iroquois helicopters, slowly buzz the air, making me dispense with the ten percent in me that might have been Jainist as I roll up a newspaper and savagely beat them to death.

Somehow summer has turned to autumn as trees go gold and red, the mornings are full of nip, and before dusk many of us still prefer to sit outside, as we did when the camp was in full stoke, enjoying the twilight calm and safety.

Pomeroy's is in full swing and was highly patronised last Friday night, so much so that all the stairs up to the Bikram Yoga studio, which is run by the publican's wife, were lined with patrons. Everyone is eager to crack a chat and there is a great deal of stoic talk about whatever SL – silver lining – people can get out of all of this. However, I must admit to a feeling of flatness, a lack of purpose, as I wonder what the point is of doing housework, or dragging a brush through my hair.

Mid week a letter arrives with a floral edge and a bag of flower seeds from a lady called Shirley, who has challenged all Shirleys to make a donation to Shirley Boys' High. She challenges me to drop some of the enclosed Love-in-a-Mist seeds as I go about my travels on the bike, and reminds me of the hope of daffodils blooming in spring.

But first there is the discontented winter to slug through as we learn patience in slower-than-a-wet-week traffic, take more orders from men in uniforms, and worry about how many have left, how many will return, and who is making the decisions for the ghosts who stayed. If you are a control freak, the kind of life we live now, with all its hold-ups and Red Zoned ruthlessness, is very hard to take. Those with initiative, who want to be up and doing and getting on with things, can't contribute to a society that badly needs impetus.

This morning I rose early to find that the power had gone out again and I wandered down to the generator to see the large container sitting there as quiet as a lamb. Three hours later it was up and running, and lo and behold three portaloos appeared in our street, even though our toilets are flushing and no floaters are turning up in the backyard.

Benecio has put on weight and isn't limping as much on his dodgy knee today. His beautiful black dinner suit has turned bear brown as he sleeps, and sleeps, and sleeps his way back to health through hibernation. Occasionally, mid stretch, the Six Million Dollar Cat (the bill came in at just under three grand) peers over at me out of his one good eye with a look that says, 'I'll make a bloody good cat out of you yet.'

Returning to brick city

APRIL 4 – A couple of days ago a freaked-out foreign student who used to live down the street in the house I named The Lost Tribe of Albinos (on account of the curtains always being drawn and no lights ever showing) returned to grab her belongings before hightailing it out of the country. She dragged everything she couldn't carry with her out on to the street, and the inhabitants down at Andrew's boarding house were elated to inform me they had scored a TV worth about a grand and a very nice selection of pillowcases and sheets.

The lovely young couple who live in the front flat at my address and work – correction, worked – in the hospitality industry in the CBD have both lost their jobs, given the landlord three weeks' notice, and are off to try their luck in Sydney. Their story is a familiar one. University students dependent on making ends meet with hospo work have abandoned hope and enrolled in other campuses. My niece, who is doing an environmental studies degree at Canterbury University, has her lectures in tents, but alas the labs are in limbo as canvas and chemistry don't mix.

Friends phone from overseas and different parts of the country to say they're coming home to bury elderly parents, who all seem to have died of heart attacks post-quake. The returned ones can't get over brick city and the proliferation of portaloos perched on every street, as out of place as Tardises.

On Wednesday I took the daily bike ride down to Beat Street Café to buy my 'militia' coffee and count the men in uniforms milling around at Checkpoint Charlie. Who should be at the counter resplendent in an orange fluorescent jacket but Robyn Malcolm, aka Sheryl West, home to lend support to her fellow Cantabs. The lads looked awestruck but voiced disappointment she wasn't sporting animal print.

While biking home I smiled at someone I took for a foreign student wearing a headscarf. She waved me down to ask where the buses were as she wanted to get to Hagley Community Centre, and I told her to go back in the opposite direction up to Fitzgerald Avenue. She motioned to the back of the bike, asked if I could dub her and hopped on the back. I thought to myself, so now I'm a rickshaw driver.

After depositing my passenger I talked to a neighbour, who said he was in 'twenty different minds about what my next move is', a sentiment to which I completely relate as my mind sings over and over again the line from *The Clash*, 'Should I stay or should I go', interspersed with the Pythonic 'Always look on the bright side of life'.

The irony is I moved into Kilmore Street a week after the September quake, hoping to enjoy a last dreamy summer in central Christchurch and the stone's throw proximity of cafés, bars, the library and Scorpio Books, all of the joys that went to make up this city, with its gentle river and the long green-haired ladies that are the willows. That is all denied to me now as whatever is left of that life is locked away in the Red Zone, munted, forever out of reach.

The dinner party has made a comeback: people cook at home and offer platonic sleepovers as the police are out in force, arresting those weaving their way home from drinking in the bustling suburbs. I meet a friend for lunch at a restaurant in Riccarton, and as we watch the waitress climb the rocky foundation I notice that the floor slopes up and down all over the place. It makes us feel wonky, as if we're in *Alice in Wonderland* and have fallen down the rabbit hole, but the proprietors are making too much money to close down and fix the place up at the moment.

Back at base, one of the Garage People drops in and we go for a drive to Corsair Bay and Rapaki to check out my favourite swimming-hole haunts, only to find that Corsair, the preferred bathing spot of bogans, has its gates closed. Further around, at Rapaki, a giant boulder dislodged from the Port Hills in the quake has bowled right through the middle of a house, completely demolishing it, and has come to a full stop on the side of the road.

The white geese that patrol the beach seem unperturbed by their new stony inhabitants and when I paddle in the water I note its warmth due to the new sulphuric activity. On the way home I try to go up Avoca Valley to buy fruit from roadside stalls but it, too, is closed off: the residents are evicted daily from eight-thirty a.m. until four p.m. as men ignite dynamite up in the hills to pre-empt vulnerable rock from coming down in the winter rains.

My friend has come up with a name for this new sense of loss and location. She calls it 'Missing Venue Syndrome'. Every impulse to go and do, go out and get, is thwarted. Those who believe the glass is half empty – the miserabilists – are having a field day, but it is hard not to let your mind turn to a time when you took for granted the splendour that was heritage.

Welcome to the normal, they tell us, but with rumours roaring that Rolleston and the ghastly gated community of Pegasus are being touted as tomorrow's centre and heart of Christchurch, those bleak soulless locales engender little enthusiasm for our brave new world.

One thing's for sure: Christchurch, always a sprawling city with many suburbs, will wind up covering an even bigger area, wherever the rebuild. I predict the return of suburban neurosis.

The kindness of strangers

APRIL 11 – In the olden days I was in the habit of strolling down to the Bohemian Café, located opposite the Avon and a majestic avenue of poplars, to indulge in a bagel and a coffee served by the charming Sue. I had been fretting about that café and its owners, so when I saw a regular patron wandering along the road leading a brace of miniature schnauzers I stopped him to see if he knew of their fate.

Apparently the Bohemian is jake but the two office buildings next to it aren't. Sue is going back nursing and her husband is trying to get a job driving trucks to tide them over. Apparently when Sue was herding the patrons out of the shaking Bohemian a customer had the audacity to bail her up mid quake to ask for a receipt, to which she replied, 'Come back and I'll fill one out for you – probably about June.'

I am on to my second courtesy car as the insurers rang to say they were going to put Mr Swift back together again. The replacement parts took a month to arrive from poor old Japan, so hopefully the mechanics won't get radiated as they toil away putting on a new roof and windscreen and smoothing out all the bumps.

I went to the letterbox one morning and was absolutely stunned to pull out a letter addressed to 'Benecio Bowron', who, always embarrassed by the limitation of his paws, got me to open it, revealing a postcard of a very handsome feline and a message from Gilly with fifty bucks enclosed and no return address.

Benecio was overwhelmed by such a kind act, but says he feels compelled to donate it to animal welfare because there are so many other pussies worse off than him. He gets better with each passing day, the scar over his left eye making him look terribly butch, and the fur growing back on his hindquarter so I won't be able to call him 'poodle leg' any more.

People are so nice. The magic letterbox has yielded tailor-made CDs, a calendar of elegant ladies in hats, a T-shirt with a dog on it, a sick bag with a picture of Wills and Kate on the front and the instruction 'Keep this handy for the Royal Wedding on April 29th', and an acid-yellow tea towel advising: 'When life hands you lemons – make a gin and tonic.'

Yesterday I went for a walk with a cobber and ended up on Stanmore Road, where they have been tearing down the main block of shops all week. Outside where Wicks Fish used to be, and where two people died so tragically, there are bunches of sad flowers hanging from the mesh.

My friend was caught short, and with no portaloos in

sight we nervously went into Tristans, famed as the roughest bar in town. It would have been churlish to use the loo and leave so we decided to buy a drink and I asked the bar lady what kind of wine they had, to which she replied, 'There's not much call for wine from our customers but we've got a cask.'

That'll do, I said, and climbed on the bar stool to hear how Tristans had become a meeting point for the traumatised community as the bulldozer continued to attack and flatten.

Tristans' owner Colleen, who looks like the third Topp Twin, arrived and related her quake story, how she had been in the car and got knocked off the Sydenham bridge and watched with horror as the building with the kiwi on top of it fell down in front of her. The early opening pub is one of the few buildings left and she is resolved to stay, but will not be signing any ghastly pledge. I quite agree, loathing The Pledge with its overtones of McCarthyism and the pledge that American evangelicals make to keep their virginity until marriage. I feel like starting a counter movement just to be perverse, inspired by *The Animals*' line: 'We gotta get out of this place, if it's the last thing we ever do.'

I have been driving Miriam to and from work as she has been relocated to one of the new business parks in Addington. It takes two buses to get there and a long stretch to the bus stop at night in semi-industrial unlit streets that are scary for a woman to walk alone. She thinks it's only a matter of time before someone gets mugged and then there'll be all hell to pay.

I go and visit Paddy, the computer guy in the east, and they're heartily sick of the trucks coming daily to blow the silt out of the drains. 'We are all of a mind for the council to cut off the water for a week and just fix it once and for all,' he says wearily.

On Saturday I drive over to Riccarton to go to Briscoes and every man and his dog is there with carts piled high, replacing what they've lost in the quake. Everyone has lists and there is no enjoyment to this kind of shopping as they trudge the lanes.

I'm moving next week to the front flat, which will be sunnier and bigger, and the padre brother will be staying with me for Holy Week before leaving for study leave in England. I tell him he's like the canary in the tunnel in reverse because every time he leaves Christchurch Old Bucky comes back to town.

Last weekend I went to Auckland for work and what a surreal experience it was too, all expensive cars, hot weather and hordes of people. I felt quite the hick and realised I kept looking for something that wasn't there. It was the piles of rubble. Over and out from Betty Rubble.

Unpeopled park

APRIL 18 – As the fire engines tear out of the Kilmore Street Fire Station and belt past my house my thoughts often turn to my great-grandfather, whose photograph rests on the mantelpiece. Back in the day when the fire carts were drawn by draught horses that were led down to the Avon River to quench their thirst, great-grandfather Stewart was the fire chief. I never met him but my mother always told the touching story of going to Christchurch Hospital after he'd been diagnosed with terminal cancer. When he heard the footsteps of his son and granddaughter coming down the hall, he piped up his customary, 'Here's someone who belongs to me.'

As they stood at his bedside not knowing what to say, my great-grandfather introduced the elephant in the room to his nearest and dearest by announcing, 'I ain't afraid of dying, Bruce and Fay. I ain't afraid of dying.'

I think I saw my mother cry only half a dozen times in my life but she always welled up when she told that story. Today I find myself staring at his straight-backed, handsome image in his fire brigade uniform, complete with medal, and feeling that his contribution is part and parcel of the mammoth effort taking place further along the road.

In May it will be three years since I came down here to reside with the Aged Parents, who both needed a live-in relative to care for them. How thankful I am that Old Bucky held off 'til they had quit the coil, as I could not imagine how they, or I, would have coped with their intense respective health needs without power or water. Even if they had been in good health, the wreckage of the city where they were born, grew up, met, courted and married (at the Sign of the Takahe) would have profoundly set them back and hastened their demise.

On a particularly sunny Tuesday I take a walk in the Botanic Gardens to admire the trees in their autumn finery and I count not seventy people passing in over an hour and a half. The park is so unpeopled it gives me some idea of how a royal must feel taking a tour of his or her grand estate and only bumping into the gardeners. Normally the place bustles with tourists and locals, particularly fit and elderly Cantabrians determined to enjoy the park and name all the plants in the herbaceous borders, but the earthquakes and the aftershocks have brought a loss of confidence.

I worry for the elderly who have had their wings brutally clipped and sit at home too scared to go out for fear of Old

Bucky returning and their getting struck down, with no one to come to their aid. Their loss of vitality, both mentally and physically, will bring a raft of problems our health system will not be able to cope with.

At last my car is ready and I drive the courtesy vehicle across to the panel beaters, past the sad silted citadel that is the AMI Stadium with its name writ large, which says it all really. I pick up Mr Swift and drive the Suzuki down St Asaph Street, past the crumbled edifice of the Community of the Sacred Name, which recently housed an order of Anglican nuns. How hard I used to stare into their windows to try and catch a glimpse of the line of white Stetson line-dancing hats that a gay friend alleged could be seen from the road. Alas, neither the hats nor the penguins are in evidence, having relocated south to Ashburton – or Ash Vegas, as it is affectionately referred to.

St Asaph Street is opened up right through now, revealing that its right side is 'futterly ucked' as locals are wont to say – 'munted' now being so last month. I cruise down Bealey Avenue to see that they've taken down the hundred-year-old Carlton Hotel. Back in the day it was a big bump-and-grind pub where our flat, full of strapping young girls, would take to the dance floor in our witches' boots, writhing to a live band, fervently hoping that our artless gyrations would attract the scrutiny of a bold deceiver. Now all that's left is a gaping hole to add to all the other gaping holes.

A trip to Leithfield Beach, where my parents spent their first night of their honeymoon, reveals that the modest shacks and bachs are now fetching prices of $200,000 plus. I swing by Rangiora, where I spent my early years, to see that the tiny service town I couldn't wait to get out of is now a throbbing metropolis, its ranks having swelled by some three thousand post quake, with house prices up thirty percent.

On the way home I call in at my brother's church to put flowers on the Aged Parents' grave, to find that yet another cordon has been erected a few feet out from the falling hall and I can't get to them. I throw the flowers over the wire netting and they land on the bricks.

The move to the front flat was in full stride on Saturday night when Old Bucky came back. Fortunately I hadn't hung any pictures on the walls and hadn't unpacked the crockery so the tremor left Benecio and me unscathed. We just stood in the middle of the room and stared at each other while I yelled, 'Is that all you've got!'

Police and members of the public help rescue people from the collapsed Canterbury Television building on Madras Street after the 6.3 earthquake, February 22. *Carys Monteath/The Press*

Corner of Barbadoes and Kilmore Streets in my neighbourhood, the day after the February 22 earthquake. *Don Scott/The Press*

ABOVE Damaged apartment building, formerly The Normal School (built 1874) on the corner of Kilmore and Montreal Streets at Cranmer Square, February 22. *Richard Cosgrove/The Press* BELOW The army in Montreal Street patrolling the inner-city cordon, February 23. *Phil Reid/The Dominion Post*

ABOVE Cathedral of the Blessed Sacrament, Roman Catholic basilica (built 1905), Barbadoes Street, February 23. *Don Scott/The Press*
RIGHT Icon of the Virgin Mary, Cathedral of the Blessed Sacrament, April 10. *Kirk Hargreaves/The Press*

ABOVE Massive slips in Redcliffs, February 24. *Chris Skelton/The Dominion Post*
BELOW Rock fall near Redcliffs School, February 27. *Don Scott/The Press*

ABOVE Volunteers of the Farmy Army, organised by Federated Farmers, arrive in Opawa with wheelbarrows and shovels to help clean up liquefaction, February 26. *Craig Simcox/The Dominion Post* BELOW Mountains of silt and sludge cleared from Wildberry Street, Opawa, March 3. *Kirk Hargreaves/The Press*

ABOVE A mountain biker negotiates subsidence on River Road, Richmond, March 12. *Barry Harcourt/The Southland Times* BELOW A brick house lies in ruins in St Martins, March 6. *Craig Simcox/The Dominion Post*

Quake porn

APRIL 25 – The Herb Centre Café where it all went down – and up and down, not to mention sideways – for me on the day the earthquake came to town is open again. I hadn't seen the waitress and chef since February 22, and although names have never been exchanged we are mutually chuffed to clap eyes on each other again. We revisit the drama of that day, how I was almost on my way to the picture framer's directly opposite, but changed my mind at the last minute and thought I'd have a coffee first. How different my fate would have been as that building dropped to the ground in seconds, the picture framer only managing to niftily escape certain death by jumping out a side door. Now I see him in the café sitting at the window staring sadly across at the space of cleared land that used to be his thriving gallery.

Business at the café isn't what it was but they're optimistic for more after announcing their comeback on the internet and doing letterbox drops round the 'hood. Picking up where I left off, I order exactly the same thing I had on the last occasion I was there – a coffee and a mixed salad – only this time the cappuccino's on the house and I get to finish my meal without the rude interruption.

I ask the whereabouts of other regulars but the waitress has no idea, and we talk of how post quake you keep looking out for people you recognised by sight who walked your route and wonder what happened to them. I guess we'll never know.

Diagonally opposite at the fire station a canvas canopy arching clear across Kilmore Street is bolted on to containers. The core of the firehouse is compromised by the two brick buildings either side of it, which were accommodation blocks, so the fire trucks are parked in the middle of the road under the canvas and the firemen are being housed next door at Foley Towers backpackers' accommodation.

'I guess that means Kilmore Street won't be opening up further any time soon?' I ask a fireman. He tells me the overhead walkway between the convention centre and the town hall is munted and there is major damage underneath the roads; water and electricity coming on intermittently is causing floods and a very real possibility of fire.

Ballantynes has flooded several times and the roads in the CBD are so fragile there's no way cars can drive in there: permanent fencing is going up to prevent any breach. Back in the 1850s Captain Thomas made maps of the small rivers and streams that run under the city. These 'black maps', housed at the Canterbury Museum, show the contours of swampland and small waterways beneath us that are now declaring themselves.

I had it in my head that the Red Zone was shrinking, healing and diminishing like a scab, but hearing this makes me realise the heart of the city really is forbidden. We talk about the massive costs of it all and he says the biggest bill will be for the repair of the water pipeline and fibre-optic cable that go from Diamond Harbour to Lyttelton. Apparently the cable is in a terrific tangle.

An old mate from up north arrives for a couple of nights and as we drive around he is completely stunned at the devastation. 'You see it on the TV but I had no idea. It's a complete write-off, a bloody ghost town.'

I realise it's a lot for fresh eyes to take in, that I've become immune, as we bunny-hop along bumpy streets and he keeps repeating, 'The roads are so stuffed – where do you start?'

As usual, nothing is ever open at Easter, but in Christchurch there really is nothing open on Good Friday. For something to do I get on the bike and ride up all the nearby streets, Gloucester, Worcester, Cashel, Lichfield and Tuam, which used to go right through but now end in a uterus at the Red Zone. Everyone else has the same idea and by the time I get to St Asaph Street, which graphically reveals the damage of the interior, the foot traffic of sightseers is so thick it's positively Mediterranean. Sure it's quake porn but people are naturally curious and I'm a bottom-liner, as in 'See how bad it is, absorb it, and then start getting on with business.' However, I fully understand those who don't want a bar of looking at any of it.

The vicar brother is staying for a few days. Even though I warned him I wasn't going to Mrs Doyle (as in Father Ted) for him, I find myself getting up at dawn's crack to slap a plate of scramblers down in front of him and hear him say, 'Highly toothsome, even better than Mrs Doyle.'

I ask him how his elderly parishioner Terry will cope when he's away on sabbatical if the locum doesn't want to do prayers twice daily with the old fellow. In his seventies and on a walking frame, Terry has apparently already breached the cordon to attend St Mary's in Manchester Street, before being collared and brought home in an army lorry.

A friend I've made down at Pomeroy's drops in at the end of Good Friday with a guitar and two new songs to try out. Vincent, the artist over the back, arrives and Miriam returns a pot. The lungs are given a workout with a few cover songs and we talk about how the quake has thrown us together, how we are all less shy about banging on a door and just wanting to hang with some one we hardly know.

It's the best thing to come out of Old Bucky but the guitarist, who's a chippie, is disturbed by what's happening with the rebuild, or non rebuild. He tells of huge scavenging going on at the transfer stations, and the wholesale taking away of native timber, and the rubbing together of hands by those selling building materials at top price. He bemoans the lack of fair play, those in the building industry not coming together for collective best practice, and the lack of governmental vision or a plan. Without power and water for months, sitting alone in a munted riverside house with no decisions having been made about it, he's had a guts-full. 'I've looked and listened to Brownlee on TV and I know he's not my friend. He's not saying anything. After the law change, if he's got the plan he should give it to us. This is a crisis. Speak from the heart, mate.'

The front flat I've moved into has net curtains. On garbage collection day, for the first time since I've lived in Kilmore Street I observe someone riffling through the rubbish bins for food.

City of once

MAY 2 – People often describe the earthquake experience as surreal but it's remarkable how quickly we have all adjusted to this 'new normal' we keep hearing about. However, I must admit I do find myself sometimes wondering if we've all died and are hanging out in purgatory, like an unseen episode of *Lost* where we have to work out our karma before going to the next level.

Friends from out of town say they want to come and see the devastation for themselves and I tell them they'd better hurry up because buildings are being knocked down, the ground made clean, and it's hard to remember what used to stand there in the city of once, as we, to use an odiously modern term, appear to be moving forward.

After the September earthquake we were told to brace and prepare ourselves for the aftershocks to come over the next year. In those days, only eight months ago, the aftershocks were small terrors that bit into your day as you ticked them off and imagined we were working through an imagined quota until time passed and things settled down. Then along came the Boxing Day twitch, which really put the frighteners underneath us and brought the realisation that if you had control-freak issues you were in trouble, big time. I remember being in Paper Plus in Cashel Street and stampeding, along with everyone else, for the door and getting knocked into shelves, my wrist in plaster, and thinking, That's not going to be terribly good for it.

Ballantynes and the Guthrie Centre opposite appeared to jump into the air and land with a great thud as I got out smartly and marched briskly home, incredibly shaken. Everyone else seemed to be just standing in the middle of the mall and taking photos but not me, I was out of that city lickety-splitty, walking past sobbing citizens routed to the spot.

After February 22 the word on the street was that the aftershocks were going to keep coming for the next two years, but now the current theory is that we should expect Old Bucky to be with us for the next fifty. It does your head in just thinking about it, but the good news is that lately, when people tell me about the last nasty jolt, I don't know what they're talking about. I embrace this new emotional deafness I appear to have developed toward Old Bucky, but touch wood as I say that, knowing I will once again, as Carole King penned, 'feel the earth move under my feet, feel the sky tumbling down, tumbling down…'.

The vicar brother has gone and I, along with his parishioners, interpret his absence as a sign that there will be another biggie as every time he leaves town we get severely dealt to. 'You're like a walking Ken Ring,' I tell him before he jumps on a plane and gets the hell out of Dodge.

EB, or the Energiser Bunny as I call her, because she's always on the go and trying to drag me out on the venueless town, pulled into the driveway on Friday night, and one of my new quake mates turned up at the door to say he was off forever. Scottish, he has been in New Zealand for five years, and has been slaving away working for EQR, fixing up damaged homes. His visa, which costs two grand a pop, comes up in November and he says he's sick of helping people and not getting anything back from this country so he's shooting through. I get where he's coming from but hate to see him go.

I take EB down to visit the Garage People and she is impressed with how much you can fit into a space, thinks it as fine an example of interstitial packing as she has ever seen. Rodney is his usual friendly self and we talk of the great experience of quake mates and special bonding and he agrees, saying, 'It's all high quality stuff, mate, you can't buy it in shops,' as he rips open another can and we reckon we should start up a new party and call it The Canterbury Party.

The inspection notices stuck to our doors are fading so much you can hardly tell any more if they are red, yellow or green. I am infused with a weird kind of energy, go dancing on Saturday night, and wish they'd open up day nightclubs so we could boogie off Old Bucky and dance the satanic twitch. With everything so sped up and the frenetic energy going down in the suburbs, people are living every day as if it were their last. I go to the supermarket and fling twenty-five dollars across the counter for a dozen Bluff oysters and congratulate myself for the indulgence. Benecio really enjoys them. His coat has become so glossy and shiny he's in danger of bringing down planes.

Orderly swilling

MAY 9 – It's pretty much been a week of bleak, blah days reminiscent of that Carpenters' verse 'Hangin' around, nothing to do but frown, rainy days and Mondays always get me down' as you try and tear a hole in the fog and get a grip. But this morning the sun has got his hat on and is coming out today as I turn on the washing machine and notice that Benecio has caught a mouse and left it neatly by the fridge, as if to say, 'Park that in there, my good woman. I'll have it for later.'

So that's what all the noise was about last night. Since his operations Benecio has done little else but sleep and eat and won't even stir himself when Miriam comes over to seek an audience with Sir, who opens one eye and looks at her as if to say, 'Wake me up in October, madam.'

On Wednesday I drove out to Rangiora, or 'Ranginui' as it is now called, due to the huge amount of displaced residents of Aranui who have relocated there. When I grew up in Rangiora it was a small service town to the farming community with a lot of weirdo religions thrown in, but now it throbs like a veritable metropolis.

I remember how my mother would slap her handbag over her wrist, grab her trundler and announce contemptuously, 'I'm just going down to the village.' In those days she scornfully told everyone that Rangiora was good only for meat and underpants; she would long for the day when she could catch the bus into town to visit her spiritual home of Ballantynes.

Having heard that looters are being processed at Rangiora I poke my nose in at the courthouse to see the bulging courtroom. The halls are lined with mostly callow youths, tails firmly between legs, as the duty solicitors conduct interviews in the middle of it all, in interview rooms full to the gunnels. The lawyers, judge and court officials look grey with fatigue. The receptionist at the office says the judge will keep slogging through until it's cleared, whatever it takes.

I bump into an acquaintance who tells me that since his home was completely munted in February he has moved three times and has been burgled twice, left stripped of everything except three changes of clothes. He was in Menlo Street, Mt Pleasant standing in his kitchen when the earthquake hit. The fridge fell on him, he managed to extricate himself, then a brick wall collapsed, breaking his toe. His house has a track that cuts down to Ferrymead. Locals, unable to use the road, accessed the track and arrived at his property up to their thighs in silt. He and they stood under a maple tree and looked down at the Ferrymead bridge, observing cars driving madder than dodgems as they disappeared into potholes. He fired up his old dunger of a van, filled it with elderly residents, and managed to navigate the ripped-up roads to enter their houses, turn off the water mains, and point them in the direction of the drinks cabinet.

When he got home he watched the arrival of an enormous red cloud of dust from the cliff drop of Redcliffs, found a bottle in the wreckage and slept in the van. His acts of kindness that day were bread on the waters as the neighbours he helped have, in turn, given him the use of dwellings so he has a roof over his head until he gets a payout for the house he had just painstakingly finished doing up.

The Energiser Bunny, aka EB, always up for it, is thrilled when I invite her to be my wingman—or wing rabbit—on a sortie to Riccarton on Thursday night to see if we can spot any of the alleged bad behaviour that has brought about an alcohol ban in that burg.

All the bars are packed, the restaurants doing a roaring trade with solid Cantabrians swilling in an orderly manner, and we wind up at The Craic, one of those bland generic Irish pubs, where EB spots a legal eagle cracking a chat with a cough crow at the bar.

Employing her usual effusive Labradorian greeting she bails him up and we hear his account of his quake day, which started in Aranui and got sidetracked to the terrors of terra firma erupting in Avonside as he desperately tried to get to his wife, who acts as his legal secretary, trapped on the

Orderly swilling

seventeenth floor of Clarendon Tower in the CBD. She had managed to get down to the eleventh floor and had to wait until firemen arrived and led her to the ninth, where the firm of Duncan Cotterill had a hitherto unknown internal staircase which took them all the way down. Having never sent a text message in his life, the legal eagle had managed to send her a clumsy text saying he'd meet her down below, greeting her as she appeared sodden from the water of the sprinklers.

A family court lawyer, he can't retrieve files from the tower and has no backup, but fortunately the courts have copies in their system. He will never return to the seventeenth. Now located in first floor premises in Riccarton, he is happy to be closer to his home and seems content in the bland sprawl. Right from the start EB reckoned all those relocated to the satellite 'burbs would dig in and never return to the centre that did not hold.

Everywhere in Kilmore Street, outside abandoned homes, dead wet mattresses that people can't give away lean drunkenly on fences. Rodney from the Garage People has a rural background and is helping me put down a proper garden as he bides time, hoping to get work on farms.

More letters arrive for Benecio from females and I tell him, 'Do I look like a pimp?' A friend phones to say he's bored with study and obsessed with going on the Pippa Middleton arse appreciation website. This gives me an idea. I tell Benecio I might do a copycat and make a Benecio Bowron poodle leg appreciation website. He bites the hand that feeds him.

Anger management

MAY 16 – With the two nasty shakes that viciously punctuated last week and put everyone two steps back, the oft heard phrases on the street are as follows: 'Did you feel that one?' 'When's it going to end? 'I'm over it.'

The upside to being an insomniac is that I was awake for both, as I was for the September original, which is a blessing: I can't think of anything more scary than being stirred from deep slumber by the intimidations of Old Bucky.

Whose fault was it – the Greendale or the Port Hills fault? – everyone asks, turning on their transistors to hear where, what magnitude, and how deep, as we listen to the talkback hosts quickly slip into quake doctor mode and calm freaked out Cantabrian callers in the pitch of the dark.

Benecio leaps off the bed and rushes out the cat door but comes back fifteen minutes later, having turned into a dog. When I get up to go to the loo he accompanies me like a John Key bodyguard; when I go to get a glass of water he trots along beside me; when I read a book he lies on the newspaper and stares down at the page as if deeply absorbed in the written word.

Wherever they came from, these last two shakes have the seismologists stumped and I'm beginning to think like a detective from *Criminal Minds* or *CSI*, arriving at the conclusion there are two Old Buckys, working together like serial killers, copycatting each other's terrible work and dividing up the province between them.

When daylight comes I notice that the cracks in the foundation have opened up even further, and I prop a stout tree branch up against the worst one in my girlie inept way, with a rock to support it at the end. When the landlord drops by to mow the lawn, to my horror I hear myself saying, 'Have you seen my crack?' and go bright pink in the cheeks. Good grief, I'll be hawking it down Manchester Street next.

After the Monday night nasty I phone an old friend and invite him to meet me down at The Fitz to have a wine outside on a trying-very-hard-to-be-sunny Tuesday afternoon. By the time he arrives I have followed the last rays and table-hopped to the front outside area, where a boisterous contingent of smokers comes out to fag up large, in between shots on the pool table.

An old wag by the name of Jonathan introduces himself and starts purloining my wine glass, but in the nicest possible way. He suffers from a chronic case of gregariousness and volunteers up his quake story, which is both funny and horrid at the same time. In his mid sixties, he is a retired painter but got roped into painting the Grand Chancellor (now called the Leaning Tower of Chancellor) and was on the twenty-third floor when the quake hit. He watched the Holiday Inn sway in front of his eyes in the manner of the Scottish song, 'Have you ever seen a lassie go this way and that? … Have you ever seen a lassie go this way and that?'

Stranded high and dry, he and his co-workers raided the minibars of the entire floor, poured some stiff ones and stared down below, watching the police write on the footpath 'Help is coming.' Jonathan raised his glass in a toast and said, 'Take your time boys'; he was craned off the fourteenth floor by four p.m. He still can't get out of his mind the image of what he saw when his feet touched the ground – two buckled dead bodies lying in the rubble.

My nephew's wife has exciting news. She has scored a fantastic job in Wellington so they, too, are quitting the city and I'm down to one niece and an aunt and uncle. I will miss them and our fortnightly meals and spirited debriefs sorely, but I am so pleased for them that they are on the up. The nephew is meeting up with his father in Spain in a couple of months' time and I hope the Old Bucky that has devastated Lorca will have thoroughly done its block by then.

Much has been written recently about how we are coping psychologically, that we have moved from the honeymoon phase, which I must have missed because nobody left a chocolate on my pillow, and that we are now in the angry phase. A Wellington friend comes through and brings a chunk of Canterbury lamb to generously give to the mutton dressed

Anger management

up as one, and remarks how grumpy people in Christchurch are at the moment.

His observation is on the money, with all of us, as a quake mate so succinctly put it, feeling like we've woken up from an operation only to discover we've had our legs amputated. That's a tad overdramatic but there is a feeling of being annexed and deleted. We have been annexed from the Rugby World Cup; we are left out of statistics about house prices; film festivals pass us by; and without an art gallery or a theatre we have become a cultural desert that stinks like yesterday's diaper. We pretend to be brave but we are fragile and brimful of real and imagined anxieties, the troubles brewing inside us centimetres from the surface.

I buy bulbs – tulips, freesias and daffodils – and plant them in pots, banking on the hope that spring springs eternal. Saturday turns on the most beautiful day that ever showed its face on Earth. I ride over to the supermarket and to my delight see a circle of house trucks and wagons and a sign saying there is a two-day gypsy fair happening in the park opposite. There is a shooting gallery. For five bucks you get twelve shots and I plum centre the cans and ducks nine out of twelve. I feel good and angry, like I did a couple of weeks ago when I went to the Ferrymead golf driving range, whacked fifty balls down the straight and came away thinking, I bet this is a billion times better than anger management.

The gypsy fair is on its last leg of a nine-month tour of the country and the stallholders have a ridden-hard and left-out-wet look about them. Their band, the Village Green, sounds

Dylanesque as I sit inside Kathleena's house truck shuffling the tarot cards, cutting them in two and waiting to hear her deliver her divinations. I can't remember a thing she says as I make out a huge black face staring at me from the sepulchral gloom of the truck and am introduced to Buster, a pit bull terrier, who watches all from a padded ledge.

The fair teems with animal life. Shetland ponies are led round by a man so short you wonder if his parentage had something to do with one of the tiny horses. A lady strolls past with a green parrot called Captain Green on her shoulder, and an enormous, long-haired orange cat called Dharma peacefully coexists alongside a gentle blue heeler called Chev. Both cat and dog are tethered on long ropes to a house truck, and Dharma jumps up on a stool to be stroked and admired as people fall in love with her and put money in a donation box.

I rush home and tell Benecio about the cat on the long rope and say I think we could do better than that. 'With your black and white tuxedo you could easily take her spot,' I say to him, but deep in my heart I know he's no traveller and when I mention the leash the look of profound disgust on his face is priceless.

No, there will be no running away with the gypsies for us this week. After all there's a winter to get through and with history in the making and a rebuild to write about, we'll bide here a while longer and circle our own wagons.

Noses

MAY 23 – Finally there is some activity at the house two doors down that lost its sides in the quake and was left the proverbial mere shadow of the gentrified edifice it once was. A collection of youths have assembled to clean up the property, making Benecio as cross as two sticks as he felt he had squatting rights there, having appropriated the place as his personal man shed, luxuriating in sunny spots among the dusty rubble, turning his shiny black and white tuxedo into a dull grey suit.

In the olden days, working from home made you aware of the noisy activity of builders and gardeners going on around you, but since Old Bucky came and left the city in such dishevelment the cacophony is acute and relentless – crash, bang, hammer and nail, as trucks and bulldozers shudder the roads – and you realise it's going to be like this for – well, years.

Friends and strangers continue to send packages: a wonderful box of homemade jams and relishes, which have been much relished, with too many rounds of toast going down the cake hole as a result of such tempting spreads; green tea from Australia; and a nosegay of dried flowers, oranges and cloves from a friend who used to be a florist. I'd mentioned to her the odiferous whiffs of fat deposits emanating from opposite the casino, out the back of a Thai and sushi restaurant and Celia Hay's cooking school, and related how a Christchurch Polytech student had told me that minutes before the quake she'd seen four grand's worth of meat being delivered off a truck and left in the hall.

Now I have been instructed to ride the streets, nosegay held to nostrils in a medieval manner. This cracks me up but it's a nice thought. Perhaps there's money in the idea. It could take on. I imagine the spectacle of burly tradesmen with nosegays swinging from their builders' aprons as they enter the Red Zone.

I book into the hair salon on the corner and when I greet my hairdresser, recapping that the last time I'd clapped eyes on her was on February 22, she looks at me blankly and says she can't remember large sections of that day. I'd actually encountered and spoken to her twice when she was wandering along Kilmore Street with her boss, and had registered their eyes as big as saucers, their hands held over shocked mouths, as streams of cars piloted by white-knuckled drivers hovered in gridlock, attempting their slow exodus.

I go to pick up my magazine at Leslie's Book Shop in Lyttelton and while I'm there drop in at a temporary café situated in The Loons theatre. There are no windows and the gloom feels Berlinesque, with upside-down lamps strung up over Formica tables and '70s couches, the furniture of choice of young groovers. It might be ten in the morning but it feels like midnight, and I half expect a cabaret artiste in an evening gown to appear and slink round the tables singing huskily.

Miriam, my neighbour, takes me out for a jaunt and we go to South Library. With the central library down and out, this has obviously now become the main going concern; we abandon the full car park and have to park streets away. Inside, every seat is taken up with people, noses in books, enjoying the free warmth and reading themselves into a happy escape.

At the supermarket, St John Ambulance have a couple of people taking blood pressure. Mine is always borderline high and I wimp past them, then come back and stick out my arm and am pleasantly surprised to find that it's nearly normal. I overhear the medics tell a relatively young guy who's had a stroke the week before to get thee to a doctor quick.

Rodney, quake mate and member of the Garage People, has scored a job painting a motor camp out of town and we are all thrilled for him. On his birthday he comes to the door with a book of poems and a card that says 'Friends forever'. I am deeply touched and wish him all the very best. Simon, also from the Garage People, nearly sent his landlord orbital when he told him that, with the decamping of Rodney, he had organised two more chaps to house in the garage, before the landlord realised he was pulling his leg.

Everyone is disturbed at the mid-week front-page news that a thirty-eight-room hotel in the Square has been comprehensively looted. We wonder, if the looters were civilians, how they managed to penetrate the highly guarded Red Zone. There is wild talk that the army boys who have just come back from Timor have had a hand in it, and gossip that all the gold has been stripped out of the jewelry shops, and all the tills in every business emptied.

Outside the Red Zone, there are plenty of houses and shops that have belongings and stock still peeking out tantalisingly. The housekeeper in us longs to rescue perfectly good stuff, but the threat of being locked up for a month before trial prohibits any impulse.

A friend drops in after visiting the SuperShed – a mecca, particularly for those living in the beleaguered east, to buy affordable secondhand goods – and says how stripped of stock it is, as it is preparing to move premises. He tells of a woman coming in and yelling out that the east has nothing "and now they're taking our SuperShed!" The enormous shop on Pages Road is moving in late May to Blenheim Road on the other side of town, which will be much harder to access on that bustling arterial route.

When the Budget is read out by Bill English in parliament, an aftershock hits. Those on HootSuite, a form of Twitter, comment that Mother Nature obviously isn't very impressed. It always seems so slobbish to have TV switched on when the sun is shining, but duty calls on Sunday with the *Rise Up Christchurch* telethon on Maori TV. I drift through the lounge in time to catch Sally Ridge and Nicky Watson and a smattering of *New Zealand's Next Top Model* competitors put on a fashion show and stalk the catwalk wearing grumpy faces, as if they've just seen twenty miles of bad road. I guess if they'd just come from a tour of the Red Zone their facial expression would be entirely in keeping.

Nine lives

MAY 30 – What bliss to have the EQC-approved heat pump installed. Benecio and I saunter around in our smalls and talk of growing orchids in the tropical heat pouring into the flat.

The highly efficient and swift-working installers patiently told me how to drive the heat pump but I am a little concerned it's drying out the eyes. Benecio drank two enormous saucers of milk after a night of toasting, and I have been advised to leave a bowl of water at the base of the pump to counteract the drying process. It's like a god that needs an offering, so I have put said water into the best bowl and muttered a prayer of thanks to the mighty heat pump.

There have been a series of Baby Buckys or Bucki going down all week, nothing really violent but just enough to remind you it'll be a long time before you dare to wear high heels again, and that you have become a woman who wears sensible shoes. I bike past Cranmer Square and notice that the old Girls' High building, Mum's old school, has been bowled and that left in its place is the now all-too-familiar bleak vacant lot, wiping away all memory of the building. It sounds crazy but I prefer the rubble – even if it is a mess it is tangible evidence of what the earthquakes have put us through – but we can't live like Miss Havishams forever, can we?

Every day you wake up and the first thought that springs to mind is Old Bucky, and how we still live on the edge. I suppose this will disappear in time, but if days go by unpunctuated by aftershocks the non-rational mind starts worrying that's a bad sign because it signifies a build-up of unreleased energy and there will be a biggie to come. Highly unscientific, but that's the way everybody's thinking.

Old Bucky is like the Smoke Monster in *Lost*: you forget about him for a minute and he comes snaking back into your life to put you in your place. It's official, I've become my mother, who had what we called a bad case of the ODs – Ominous Dreads – and was always warning of pending dangers. Oh well, as a friend says it's only natural we should turn into our parents and people should be more relaxed about becoming their mother.

I have dinner with my neighbour, who has no glasses left post quake so the wine is served up in elegant little matching cups and saucers as we clink and think the trend might catch on. We go for a walk down to Latimer Square and on the way notice that a makeshift day shelter knocked up to house the Australian police who were over here at the beginning of the siege has been parked in a vacant lot. On the outside of the frame are a series of messages that are a touching part of our city's history. There's one from a sergeant of the Victoria Police saying 'Happy to help out our bros in NZ', another from a sergeant of the NSW Police saying 'Glad to have a hand in helping out a mate. What a great country', some comedian saying 'Me feeling sheepish', and another remarking 'Happy to continue the Anzac bond'. The date on the messages is 2.3.11. We hope they are preserved and someone sees to it that they wind up in Te Papa.

We get talking to a beautifully dressed elderly woman who tells us she lived in her Latimer Square home for fifty-eight years, but due to structural damage now lives with her children. She is clutching a box of dried cat biscuits and has just driven across town to leave out some food for a cat with the unpretentious name of "Puss", who still fur-patrols the property. I hope he's all right in the winter.

More of Kilmore Street has opened up and that enables me to check out the badly damaged Oxford Terrace Baptist Church, which seems to have radically deteriorated since February 22 and looks quite beyond repair, the props that held it up now part of the overall muntage.

The casino is open. I avoid the crush of night but, like one of the three little pigs, rise early in the morning to have a gander and am the only female in a largely young Asian crowd. I got over my nasty blackjack habit years ago, and walking round the floor I wonder what held me here when, full of delusion, I fancied myself as something of a card sharp. However, the casino has given me a 'Players' card, which amuses me: if produced at the Grand Café it gives you a hefty discount on the all-you-can-eat buffet breakfast, and ten percent off veges at the Raewards stores.

With sport and recreation outlets and grounds so severely compromised, people have taken to throwing a football around or playing hockey and tennis on the street, something I haven't seen happen for years and which reminds me of my childhood.

As the Rugby World Cup approaches, the hostelries that are open are beefing up their count of television screens. The oppression of wall-to-wall rugby does not excite me and I wonder why we can't go the other way and advertise Christchurch as a rugby-free mecca, a refuge from the overbearing national pursuit?

On a walk down to the café I notice a nice old cove, name of Alec, roaring down the road on his motor scooter like a geriatric boy-racer, bunny-hopping the bumps in the footpath; boing, boing, he artfully bounces along, having risen at five-thirty a.m. to get to mass over in Manchester Street.

I've noticed that people have stopped talking about leaving Christchurch and you get the feeling the hard core has settled in to stay. After all, in such a small country and a tiny population it's not as if we have, as the Americans do, a sprawl of fifty-two states to choose from and reinvent ourselves in.

I talk to a friend who says how mad he is feeling. I say, yup, I'm with you on that one, and we joke in black gallows' humour about how they'll be putting up traffic lights at Godley Head next for all the leapers.

Someone tells me the moon is drifting away from the Earth at three centimetres a year, the sun is expanding, the planet is volatile, and we have been among the underdogs to feature in the natural order, or rather disorder, of things. I reassure Benecio I don't want to be an underdog, not even an overdog, or any sort of dog for that matter, I want to be a cat, because they have the nine lives. He looks at me witheringly for being so slow arriving at this conclusion.

A short history of tractors

JUNE 5 – Early in the week we had set off for a jaunt to the Botanic Gardens and had just crossed the bridge on Barbadoes Street when my neighbour and I spotted two guys on tractors taking a break from mowing the lawn by the river. Their machines were aligned in perfect diagonal, nose-to-nose symmetry as they enjoyed their smoko and I asked if we could take a photo. They were city council workers and cheerfully announced that they were still tending the gardens in the Red Zone 'to keep on top of things'. One of them, perhaps prescient about the uproar to come after the image of council workers tending municipal gardens in the zone was splashed all over the media, immediately shot off his tractor and ran towards the river, declining to be photographed.

We were walking on towards the corner of Madras Street when a bus suddenly appeared around the corner of Latimer Square and we both shot an arm up, pointing at it and crying like four year olds, 'Look at the bus!', realising we hadn't seen one in our neck of the woods for many a moon. When it cruised past us our hearts sank as we saw normal transmission had not been resumed: the bus was chartered and full of the usual crew, men in fluoro jackets and hard hats.

As we barrel toward the shortest day we cannot growl about the superb weather we have enjoyed, having not had to resort to heavy-duty woollens or possums to keep the cold at bay. On Monday I accompany the Energiser Bunny to the Ferrymead Heritage Village with five of her special needs students. It's a weekday so the historic town is eerily deserted, mirroring the streets of the inner city back in the real world. We poke our noses into the jailhouse, haul madly on the water pump and laugh our heads off like drains, something I haven't done much of lately.

Tuesday turns into percentage day as we hear how there is a one in four chance of getting another major visit from Old Bucky. It's all everyone can talk about for the rest of the week, until a Friday night news bulletin announces there's a ruddy big fault line a stone's throw away in Barbadoes Street. Thanks very much.

I flip the calendar over to the next month, to another fetching page of the gorgeous calendar sent by my Wellington neighbour, and it occurs to me that time doesn't really matter any more as our year in Canterbury began not in January but on February 22, while last year stopped on September 4. Queen's Birthday looms and I try to book a place out of town for a mentally healthy night away, but alas, all the joints have been quake-struck or are going through major refurbishments.

Got to do something, so, bugger the expense, EB and I decide to take a six-minute, ninety-dollar ride in a helicopter over the city. As Russ, the pilot, swings us over the CBD we peer down hard at the wreckage. He points out the landmarks, including his house: 'And there's Russ's house and I see the wife hasn't put the washing out yet.' The basilica, with one dome still intact, is easy to spot but the cathedral in the square without its – and I swore I'd never use this word – iconic spire is much harder to make out, and when I finally spot it and see it literally brought so low it's a very humbling moment.

The high point of the week has been the mail, with a specially designed, earthquake-proof, silk-screened lamp constructed of polypropylene arriving from the Boatshed Gallery, which is just the ticket, as Old Bucky took out three lamps and I loathe overhead lighting – so unflattering to a woman of a certain age.

Sorry to bore you with my DNA but I think I mentioned a while back how my great-grandfather was the fire chief back in the days when the fire engines were horse-drawn. To my delight I open a large envelope to find a dramatic black and white photograph of the Christchurch fire brigade dated 1900–02, with six bewhiskered firemen standing erect on a cart drawn by two draught horses. The photograph, sent by one Dick Appleyard, was taken by J.N. Taylor and won a worldwide photographic competition, and you can see why. In the background are my favourite Christchurch trees, not the longhaired green ladies, the willows, but the poplars by what I believe is Oxford Terrace by the river. I place this stunning snap on the mantelpiece by the photograph of great-grandfather in his fire chief uniform and swear I see a smile flit across his handsome features.

I also get an amusing letter from John Peters of Wairarapa wanting to know what the next lines are of a childhood verse I quoted to describe my hygiene in the early days of the water-short siege – 'Dan, Dan, dirty old man, washed his face with a frying pan, combed his hair with the leg of a chair'. I am happy to report there is only one more line: 'Desperate Dan, dirty old man'.

My mate Bob brings round a special edition of the University of Canterbury magazine, dated 2010, with an article written after September and before February, in which two structural engineers from the university voice their concern over the post-September complacency that buildings had survived so well. They cite Chile, which had a quake in 1985 where most of the buildings survived. They rested on their oars and did nothing to strengthen their building code and when a more severe earthquake hit in 2010 there was a serious loss of life. You can bet your bottom dollar that them two profs are doing a lot of I told you sos.

Tumbleweed days

JUNE 13 – After dinner last Monday night I ventured over to Merivale to watch the tear down of Quinns fashion emporium, situated in the main drag of the posh suburb. It must have been a bitter blow for the shop owners, but as I stood there watching the digger driver artfully demolish the shops, I imagined the collective sigh of relief emanating from the husbands of Merivale, secure in the knowledge that the mighty Quinns is, for now, a mere shadow of its former self.

Ever since late February, when Old Bucky shook the shop frontage and tore down its sides, leaving it exposed like Muppet opera boxes, row upon row of shoe boxes have worried to distraction many a female passer-by, hating to see good leather go to waste. A couple of days pre-demolition a cherry picker turned up and plucked said boxes from the second floor, spoilsportedly whisking them off to the insurers for sale.

I stand next to the digger-driver's dad, who is terribly proud of his son's efforts, fondly remembering him playing with his Tonka toys in the sandpit, rehearsing for the job he would take up later on in life. Apparently things had slowed down since CERA took over from Civil Defence: the driver has five diggers sulking in his yard, desperate for action stations.

Lights have been set up across the road, a crowd has gathered, and I wonder if digger-drivers ever suffer from performance anxiety as a man gives the driver a clap when the grader comes to a standstill and I fight an infantile urge to ask for an autograph. With so many movie theatres and sports facilities down, this is what we do for entertainment these days. I marvel at the profusion of wires and the complexities of construction as the buildings are comprehensively deconstructed, and wince when some very nice French doors become collateral damage, crushed in the general carnage.

I am still reeling from the news that my uncle died last week, and selfishly interpret his going as another piece of my father quitting the coil, another chink in the personal heritage disappearing into the ether. There will be no funeral. I feel in limbo and find myself driving out to CBS Arena on Wednesday to see the Dalai Lama and wait in a line outside, feeling the bitter wind bite through my clothes. They call His Holiness a rock star and I look around to see what sort of crowd this rock star has pulled. The women have long hair and purple- and saffron-coloured scarves artlessly flung about their personages, and the men wear versions of Christ's feet shod in muddy-coloured footwear.

Tumbleweed days

When we get inside I wait patiently for about half an hour and then ask an usher in suitably hushed and reverential tones when she thinks the Dalai Lama will put in an appearance. When she tells me kick-off isn't for another hour I toss in the towel (or scarf) and walk out. After all, I saw the Dalai Lama a few years ago in Wellington. I was staggered at the simplicity and obviousness of his message and wanted to make sure I hadn't missed something vital, so I can understand why so many find solace in his utterances.

I am out all day and return to the flat at night to find Benecio has missed me. He is all over me like a cheap suit, leading me to believe absence makes the fur heart grow fonder. I talk about spirituality with him, about how my uncle was a humanist, and how I find it difficult to believe in anything, except, perhaps, Old Bucky. That wrecking ball is very real, a dramatic force in the natural world, and I suppose this may make me a pantheist. Benecio vehemently rubbishes the idea and tells me I'm a puss-tafarian through and through as I comb the dreadlocks out of his fur, admire his healed leg and tell him we'll have him kicking footballs with it before the week is out.

I attend the Energiser Bunny's birthday bash and hear how an accountant will be allowed back into his premises next to the PGC building for the first time since the quake via a cherry picker. His wife says he has the whole procedure planned with military precision, and EB, desperate to get in on the action, offers to help as I wonder how big she thinks the platform of a cherry picker is.

We talk about the Red Zone and how Rachel Hunter's visit has put paid to further celebrity and media tours, and dream up madcap schemes for getting through Checkpoint Charlie Berlin Wall-style, with incredibly low cars, a double suitcase carried by a person each side, or Hogan's Hero tunnelling.

Every other day I bike around the circumference of the Red Zone. Today I discovered you can enter the now very bulldozed and cleared bottom of Colombo Street and turn right past the town hall and the convention centre. The numbers of quake tourists seem to have dwindled, making the streets even more eerie, full of ghosts and shadows, as we live under the dictatorship of overlords who constantly assure us they know what's best for us. Birds have begun to make nests in the gables of churches and fly out of the damaged al fresco ceilings as they enjoy their new stone trees. I go down to the Garage People for a couple of drinks and they tell me they can't understand why the Dalai Lama failed to seek an audience with them.

No one talks about how we haven't had any aftershocks since the turbulence that was last Monday as to do so will bring bad luck and only encourage Old Bucky to lash out again. In my travels I note that someone or ones have meanly vandalised the temporary construction that once housed the Australian police. The poles that bore the poignant messages from the Aussies who came to lend a hand have been removed and the black polythene left sagging on the ground.

Walking round the deserted streets of Avonside and Dallington and seeing the few good houses still standing on unmangled land I wonder, if these suburbs are written off, will the remaining residents have to leave too? Will the council bother, or have the resources, to service dots of viable houses with sewage, rubbish collection, all the structure that goes to supporting a community? Wild flowers and weeds grow everywhere and add their own wistful beauty. All that is missing is the tumbleweed.

The whites of our eyes

JUNE 14 – So it's a day after the Monday noises to add to the roll-call of quakes – September 4, Boxing Day, February 22 and now June 13. I suppose a bloody good numerologist could add up those numbers and come up with something interesting.

Who knows, maybe it's all in the way you hold your mouth, but from what I've seen the general population of Christchurch is pretty down right now. Gone is the chin up, glass half full, we will rebuild, chipper stance of those who have remained. Heads are down and no eyes meet as people scurry out and get what they need to start reassembling their haciendas, digging them free of liquefaction and sweeping up the glass.

It was a one-in-four chance of getting six of the best and we got that belt straight from the headmaster, arriving swiftly after the 5.5 teaser. I was at the airport when the teaser came through and was worried my car might have been pancaked in the multi-level car park. After liberating the Swift I was driving along Barbadoes Street when Old Bucky did his block; the car felt as if it had turned into a James Bond vehicle: the tires had turned fat, bloated and become amphibian.

Back at home there was minor mess and a reunion of most of the backyard gang and a couple of other ring-ins as we gathered in the front flat. Fortunately I had laid a few botts down in the wine rack for the visitor, had changed the water in the containers just that morning, and was able to produce small savouries from the freezer to heat up, so great was the scoffing and quaffing thereof.

As each aftershock hit we dug our fingers into the armrests like girlies on a roller coaster for the first time and saw the whites of each other's eyes. That night Benecio crawled into bed for under-the-duvet therapy. I woke in the early hours before the 4.7 hit and wondered where the snoring was coming from. I looked over and saw Sir was breathing heavily as his head rested on the pillow. I pulled the flannelette sheet up to his neck, praising the fur god for sending me the marvel that is Benecio.

This morning I got on the blue pony and peddled down to see that the Basilica was looking much the worse for wear, as was every building in serious trub pre this quake. I rode down St Asaph Street and the environs and noted the lack of traffic and the businesses up and running – a Peaches and Cream sex shop, two cafés, and three panel beaters. Says it all really.

The Energiser Bunny's house on the hill in Scarborough was a riot of furniture and mess within. She needed assistance so my Auckland visitor obligingly piled into the car and we gingerly drove over through Sumner, where the cliffs looked as raw and sore as eczema, revealing considerably more slippage and what appeared to be part of a house in the rockery at the bottom. We had an hour or so to spend putting EB's rooms to rights and then got the hell out of that scary neck of the woods as fast as the Swift's little fat legs could carry us. The estuary had swollen boils of liquefaction dotting it, and waiting at the base of the deeply compromised cliff faces for the Stop sign to turn to Go was deeply unsettling.

We struck out to look for provisions for the night over in Stanmore Road towards the Edgeware end, and snaked through streets of mud where all hands were to the pump, pushing wheelbarrows through streets wide and narrow, crying liquefaction alive, alive-o. So back to square one down here, but there is a certain rhythm to it as I think fondly of early afternoon and all the quake mates turning up to ask if we're okay, of how we find joy and comradeship in each other's company, and realise we can do this, we're old hands. Bloody Benecio slopes off and in the early morning I wake the others crying out his name in the yard as they try and sleep into the late a.m.s on their impromptu Old Bucky-given holiday.

Millie has gone to Chicago for a Lego conference and I am in charge of two other cats – the gregarious Toby and the phantom Sue, who has showed herself to me only three times in the nine months I have been here. The moggies sorely miss Millie and I have promised to give them kisses and hugs, but every time I do so I look around – and guess who is watching and giving this cat-farmer a filthy look?

Texts come in from my brothers in Australia and Britain and a nephew about to get on the ferry to Wellington. Yes, I am fine, I fumble back – as my father would say, 'all parts taking equal strain' – and enjoy the brilliant sunshine the day has brought, reminding me of the bizarrely sunny day after September 4.

It's good to be alive. Sure, we are living on the edge, and when I agree to speak to Sean Plunket on his Newstalk ZB show and he asks me twice why I'm still down here, I tell him I'm down here because this is where my work is: I feel I am committed to reporting on the quake age. I don't go into the other reasons I have for not getting the hell out. I have deep roots here – four generations on each side, my parents, now resting in the grave, and a feeling of needing to see this thing through. I don't regret an Old Bucky bar of it.

Waiting for Gerry

JUNE 20 – I have always wondered what the end of the tether looks like and now, after Monday's double visitations from Old Bucky, I think I've seen it. The end of the tether is sandbanks lining the Avonside riverbank, put there in case the river, already swollen with burst water mains and raw sewage, rises with the predicted rain.

The end of the tether is in the grey faces of the men who continue against all odds to service this broken city, painstakingly blasting the water pipes free of silt, digging the hideous liquefaction out of roads and properties, endlessly plugging and repairing the roads, and scaling cliffs and tall buildings, trying to put Christchurch back together with what seems like vinegar and brown paper, as Old Bucky snickers with contempt and swings back to have another go.

The end of the tether is in the animals – in my case the three cats I'm currently in charge of – who refuse to come inside after Monday and dart into the house only to get food and whip out again. Toby, a once stroppy adolescent cat, now meows piteously. I go to stroke and utter reassurances and calm him down and spot Benecio seething, giving me the filthiest look as he turns his back and stalks off in high dudge over to Miriam's with his tail of woe.

The strong feeling is that there will be an announcement sometime later this week about which suburbs or parts of suburbs are to be retired, even though Gerry Brownlee, the earthquake minister, steadfastly refuses to be drawn on when that vital information will be released. Brownlee defends the delay, saying they have to get it right, that the insurers and reinsurers and twelve agencies are all working together furiously to make sure that, when the marching orders are given, there's a decent package to sweeten the blow.

My apologies to T.S. Eliot, but the east of Christchurch more than mutters with retreat as you go through certain half-deserted streets, the city brought to a standstill like a patient etherised on a table. I say that because earlier in the week TV3's John Campbell put it to Brownlee that the residents living in the east of Christchurch were like sick patients, simply wanting to know from their doctor what the prognosis was.

The Campbell analogy is a good one. There is a feeling Christchurch has become an impatient patient, left in a bed and put in isolation while hordes of specialists circle, assuring the patient a diagnosis is imminent, but in the meantime you can lie there and rot and worry.

The worry and the fear are the thing, and it doesn't help when people who haven't lived through the quakery keep asking, 'Why don't you just get out?' – the inference being that we're loose in the roof. Imagine if the east of Christchurch isn't viable any more, and all those thousands and thousands of residents up sticks and come to your town, your city, compete for your job, put pressure on your schools, hospitals and fragile infrastructures – what will you say then?

And for those with the will to stay, what of the developer-owned land that is earmarked for the new suburbs? Will CERA, the Canterbury Earthquake Recovery Authority, armed with its immense and sweeping powers, make sure the developers don't drip-feed the land to get top dollar? If there were ever a time for an overlord to act like one it's about now, as every time I hear the CERA word I am afflicted with the brain worm of the Dylan line:"Sara, Sara, so easy to look at, so hard to define."

It's not pity we're after down here in Christchurch, it's empathy and support, and fortunately loads of out-of-towners have that in aces. I like to rise early, around five, to get a handle on the day and was sitting in my Dad's old chair on Wednesday morning waiting for dawn when I got a hell of a fright at the sound of something large giving birth through the cat door. To my astonishment and pleasure the courier had delivered me a patchwork quilt of rich reds, browns and golds, with a note hand-stitched into a corner, 'For Jane and Benecio, to keep you both warm, June 2011', and a card written by the quilt creator, Karen Simcox, who had enclosed a picture of her cat, Charlie Rose, encased in a similar quilt pulled right up to his neck. Talk about damp-eyed.

Another day I am surprised by a knock at the door and a visit from Shirley Goss, who had written to me after the February quake and mentioned she was heading down this way to go to her Uncle Barney's one-hundredth birthday. And here she is, and her cousins, who all pile into the sitting room and we raise a glass.

Continually I have to pinch myself at the kindness of strangers and all that has happened. When the adrenaline induced by Monday's upsets wears off and I have dispatched my visitor on her plane, ash and all, I feel profoundly glum and quiet, and regret having committed to Friday night and an auction for Christchurch businesses.

The Energiser Bunny accompanies me and is astounded that I have arranged this out-of-character outing, but like everyone else there I wanted to go out and let down my hair in a different venue, which in this case happens to be a car showroom. A Mercedes, priced at one hundred and seventy grand, goes for one hundred and fifty, there is good wine, bands, and the women in attendance are dressed to the nines in their High-Street-that-was finery and impaled to the floor in heels so high they'd make ACC weep.

Sure, this is only a glorified car yard, but the scene makes me think of *War and Peace*, when the aristocracy partied on in the Winter Palace in St Petersburg as the cannons could be heard only a few miles away, signalling the approach of Napoleon's forces.

When I leave I walk along Moorhouse Avenue to flag down a taxi and happen upon a woman weeping with distress from a derailed romantic encounter. I have a feeling of déjà vu, of walking along this same stretch of road a million years ago when I was sixteen with a weeping friend as we struck out to the Hagley Nurses' Home, currently undergoing the wrecking ball treatment. What happy salad days then, spending weekends parked up on the floors of my three student nurse friends' rooms as I tried in vain to beg my father to let me leave school and train as a nurse. Alas, he took a dim view of the nursing life, thought nurses smoked too much and led wild lives, and told me in no uncertain terms that I had two choices – teaching or marrying a sod buster.

Deep freeze

JUNE 27 – Orange, red, white and green – in the good old days they were simply colours or *Cluedo* characters. Now they are statements about peoples' lives. When I hear someone, myself included, ask 'What colour are you?' it sounds impolite, discriminatory even. Kermit the Frog sang a song about how it wasn't easy being green, and I find myself feeling guilty that I'm living in a rented green-zoned house. For the orange people in the hold zone their lives remain in limbo, waiting like that unfortunate character Winnie in Samuel Beckett's *Happy Days* as she becomes literally buried in a mound of dirt.

Sick and tired of being given the mushroom treatment, left in the dark for months by CERA, at last those in the red zone have been offered a deal, but one doesn't envy them purchasing land off greedy developers, borrowing heavily from the banks to afford land in the west, and battling with insurance companies over the ghastly fine print.

The enormity of moving entire neighborhoods to greener pastures is mind-boggling: there is talk of streets with strong bonds forged post quakes moving en masse. You wonder if the government is prepared for a resistance movement from those who may dig their feet in and absolutely refuse to budge, choosing instead to stay on, tap into the national grid, and keep using the chemical toilets – or, as friends joke, bring back the night cart man, he who used to visit houses back in the 1920s to collect the human waste.

The announcement – only the day after Thursday's big announcement – that red-zoned land will be bought by the government, eventually redeveloped, and then put back on the market years down the track made those in the red flinch. As they grapple with their brave new world, they wince at the notion of others one day living where they had so confidently put down roots before being moved off their land.

It is the old, the fiercely – as they say – independent who desperately want to keep living where they have grown up, married and bred, and from where they hoped to be carried out in a box, whom you fret for. At the beginning of the week a quake mate and I got to visit an old-timer called Joseph, who is pushing ninety-four and living in one-room rented accommodation in a once grand old house in the inner city. There's a single bed, a kitchen sink, and a sash window through which he stares out as he sits at the table listening to the blare of his radio. The stud in the room is ten feet high; when his heater packed up for ten days he called the room 'the freezer'.

Deep freeze

After February's quake, Joseph, who depends on Meals on Wheels, didn't get a visit from the service for a month. He's currently having problems with his pre-pay 'power manager', and hasn't had a shower for a long time as the hot-water cylinder has been out of action since November. When I ask him what he likes to watch on his TV he says he can't watch it because of his bung eye. He'll get a good wash when he goes into St George's Hospital to get the cataract removed.

Since the February quake he hasn't been this side of Barbadoes Street and has absolutely no interest in seeing the Red Zone or the devastation of the city. 'What's the use? I've seen enough,' he says, having observed the wreckage of Stanmore Road, where he walks to post his mail.

He's been in Christchurch for all the quakes, but says June 13 was the worst because he was holding on to a water pipe outside his house and it felt like 'the barrage of Alamein when 180 guns went off at one time and you could see it across to Alex [Alexandria] with the water shimmering with the percussion of the guns'.

A packet of Holiday cigarettes sits among the general clutter of the table but he insists he doesn't smoke, he only puffs, an activity he has indulged in since his early teens, he tells me, as he stares fixedly out the window and I ask him what he thinks about. 'Dreamtime,' he says. He tells of being made a ward of the state at the age of ten, when he was split up from his sister, whom he never saw again. He heard news of her a while back, when she was in her eightieth year and living in Pakuranga, but he never actually laid eyes on her.

He joined the army under age and we look at the medals on the uniform he keeps in pristine shape in his wardrobe, and hear about all the wonders he saw in the war years. 'Memories,' he says, 'that's all you've got', and takes another puff.

While we're there a Meals on Wheels lady turns up with tinfoil-enclosed tucker. Joseph thanks her, dutifully writes the date on the outside, and puts it in his fridge with all the other meals. When he stands up to cross the room I see how frail he is, and after I leave I keep thinking of him getting up in the middle of the night and walking outside across a covered way to the toilet in the freeze of the night.

A kind soul at the Linwood Community Centre has lent him a heater until his other one comes back from being fixed. God knows what the power bill will be. I read about the Red Cross Earthquake Commission offering power grants for the elderly living in damaged houses, but you have to go online to get one. When I ring the commission and point out that many of the elderly don't use a computer, I am assured they can send out a form. The grant ends on Monday so it won't help Joseph. He's begun to talk of going into care as he finds it baffling coping with the power manager cards and not having a phone.

It's been a rainy, soggy week but toward the end of it I get out the blue pony and go for a ride through the park, and notice with shock that although it isn't even July the daffodils near the band rotunda are up and showing small clenched faces.

Deep freeze

I drive out over to the estuary and see, blistering the water at low tide, all the mounds of liquefaction that will kill off the food supply to the bird life. God knows what the godwits will think when they arrive from their annual pilgrimage and find no nourishment to greet them at the end of the mammoth journey. We'll have to make up food parcels and leave them dotted along the shore so they don't go home and bad-mouth us to the other godwits, I tell Benecio, who nobly offers to help with the distribution.

It took until the end of June for winter to really be upon us. What is left of the populace has dusted off the puffer jackets favoured by Cantabrians. Lorraine from the Garage People suggests we have full bodysuit puffer jackets and space helmets made up, so if Old Bucky comes back again we will have suitable armour for protection from the falling rubble.

I trawl back through sent and received messages on the cell phone over the last few months and see 'R U OK?' writ large a million times. It's a wonder this cut-to-the-chase question hasn't wound up on emblazoned across T-shirts.

Cracking up

JULY 11 – I was out for a blat on the bike on Wednesday afternoon when I got to the corner of Manchester and Kilmore Streets and was stopped in my tracks by the strange spectacle of a huge peeked roof suspended in the air by a massive crane. Father David Moore, the vicar of St Luke's in the City, stood on the footpath behind the cordon grimly watching the grader driver gnawing away at the final brick columns supporting the roof of his church, and said how much he wished it were all over. The church had been waiting since April for the demolition to be approved and now it was finally happening.

I commented on the great care the grader driver was taking knocking the last walls over to liberate the kauri roof from the building and Father Moore nodded, saying there was something 'strangely admirable in a sickening kind of way' about the tenderness of the operation.

Cracking up

Every day in central Christchurch is another D (demolition) day, but when the roof finally detached itself from the building there was a great creaking of wood, similar to the sound you might expect to hear on an old sailing ship, as it finally swung free and hung dangling in the sky, like a whare that had suddenly ended up in a Salvador Dali painting.

'Thar she blows,' someone in the crowd said, as the demolition men, looking very Lilliputian, scattered underneath, scrambling for the guy ropes fixed to strops on the slate roof as they worked to manipulate the roof into the tight space allocated on the ground.

Meanwhile, two men jumped into a cage and were busy being levered up by another crane, to lodge between the nave and the last piece of church building still standing, when one of them took out a knife and slashed the rope free, a demolition midwife cutting an umbilical cord.

A small wind blew up and the roof responded, swinging around in the wrong direction until the men rushed to pull on the ropes as they calculated, heaven knows how, the position point on the ground. The crane gently started to winch the roof down, trying not to damage the rich pickings of slates on the roof – five dollars each second-hand, twenty-eight dollars new.

Not so fast: two young trees that had just progressed to teenagehood were in the way. A chainsaw screeched the air and hacked through their trunks, cutting them off in their prime. Finally the roof was laid to rest, brought low and kneeling by the rubble of the church, making it look like something a latter-day Noah might have fashioned for his ark.

Perched on a lamp post observing all this, a paradise duck kicked up a hell of a squawk, as if to say, 'Excuse me but I had a nice nest going on in that roof.'

So another fine historic church bites the dust, adding to the demise of all the other historic buildings that contributed to this very English of cities, created by Edward Gibbon Wakefield, whose intent it was to establish here 'a vertical slice of English society'. And that is exactly what flourished until Old Bucky came and knocked the Midsomer out of us, so that Cantabrians can no longer take delight in treating tourists to a little bit of England on the opposite side of the world.

The new inner-city of Christchurch that is going to be built won't resemble the old country, and you wonder if the new city and its changes will bring about a quiet revolution and put a stop to that curious obsession of laying claim to the most tenuous link with those who came out on the first four ships.

Remember the good old days after September 4, when the topic for weeks was the tear down of Manchester Courts? That wasn't even a year ago but the fever-pitched efforts from heritage supporters to preserve that building now seem absurd, with so many buildings for the wrecking ball and others waiting for it like the grand old Duke of York's men, 'neither up nor down', 'til the paperwork's done.

And remember the good old days after February 22, when the letters page of *The Press* rang with missives imploring the powers that be for a walk through the Red Zone? After June 13, no one's asking for that because it's sunk in that we live in dangerous times, that the goalposts keep moving with the ground, that we can't ever, in the words of the Beatles, 'get back to where we once belonged'.

News that Show Week will be in November as usual, and that there is still an imperative for Cashel Mall to be up and running by then, seems unbelievable. For those who were there for Boxing Day and for February 22, that particular stretch of the road is known as the killing fields, no matter how many compromised buildings are knocked down. Even if Show Week goes ahead and out-of-towners flock to the city, where will they stay?

We thought we had purchase, a grip on our city and the land, but now we are unsure as the town hall, the conference centre, the AMI Stadium, the library – a whole swag of public and private buildings, and acres and acres of residential land – remain uninsured. We ask ourselves: Is the city viable?

Living among long-term constant destruction takes its toll on the populace. We fall quiet, find our own routines, share new routes to take through and around the city as roads open up and close off again. You stick with those you went through the quakes with. You turn to the crew who were in the lifeboat with you for comfort and sanity, and to draw assurance that your strange angers, fears and fatigues are a common experience. The self-checking reminds me of my Alzheimic mother when she asked me, 'How do I be a person?'

While the exodus continues of those zoned red who want to take their chances in new fields, there will always be those who stay regardless, because of the networks, good and bad, in this city. I am addicted to going out on the bike to observe the ever-changing and disappearing terrain, and crack up laughing at a sign, 'You crack me up', which someone has written over a deep fissure in a footpath. If Basil Brush were around, he would write 'Boom boom' underneath.

Life in the fridge

JULY 18 – We had just got on the Ballantynes bus to Timaru when a fellow traveller came down the aisle and asked if we were with the fire service group. 'No, we're with the mongrel mob,' I replied.

As we pulled out of Burnside Park at nine of a Sunday morning, Anne, the extremely affable bus guide, accessorised to the max and made up expertly like a porcelain doll, teased us by asking if we wanted to stop off at Dress Smart for two hours, while Graham, the driver and only male on the bus, alleged it was his first trip to Timaru – 'So don't be surprised if we end up in Picton.'

We had chosen a spectacularly sunny day for the journey, but the frost that morning had been particularly white and crunchy, leaving our trotters as frozen as ice blocks. Anne assured the packed bus that logs would be thrown on the fire in a jiffy and we'd soon warm up, as a chorus of 'Put another log on the fire, fix me up some bacon and some beans' started up. Good grief, singing on the bus already and we'd only just pulled out of the car park.

Our host informed us that throughout the morning we would be treated to talks from guest speakers – that is, staff members who had been ringbolting from Christchurch to Timaru many times a week since February 22; they would be happy to take their turns to tell us about products.

Anne said 'our French girl – she's from France' would teach us how to pronounce French apparel labels. We made a great meal of exaggerating the syllables written out phonetically for us: Croisillon to Kwaz-ee-on, and so forth. Another staff member delivered a talk about the longevity of different types of pillow, and passed around paper and pencil, instructing us to draw a pig for a personality analysis. If you drew your pig at the top of the page you were a positive thinker. If your pig had no legs you were stupid. The length of your pig's tail was commensurate with your sex life.

By the time we piled off the bus at Ashburton for a comfort stop, Graham had been awarded the French name Gigi and was dispensing free ankle rubs to ladies still complaining of cold feet.

All this for twenty bucks there and back, with lunch thrown in and a couple of glasses of bubbly on arrival – talk about goodwill and value for money. I had never been to Ballantynes in Timaru. Finding it an exact replica of the Christchurch store only smaller was like reuniting with the proverbial long-lost chum.

Life in the fridge

How well I remember as a child making pilgrimages to the Christchurch store with my mother to choose material and a Simplicity or Butterick pattern, perching on the tall beige stools as the lady in black sent the docket and money up the shoot to the change department, from whence it shot back down again.

All the rites of passage took place at that emporium: meeting Mum after school in the plush green lounge downstairs before getting fitted for the first bra; selecting the first make-up; sauntering round the china department, whispering of Spode; and descending into the bowels of the building to spend a penny for the privilege of splashing your boots in a posh store.

Anne told us we had three hours to shop up large: a forklift would be on hand to feed our purchases into the bus's hold, and if we came back with bags that did not carry the Ballantynes' logo, they would happily look the other way.

Before the Ballantynes store in Christchurch closed abruptly at the end of February, only two trucks of merchandise were regularly dispatched to Timaru. Now the number has swelled to nineteen to cope with the demand from Cantabrian shoppers. All going to plan, the store will reopen on October 29 with a much smaller footprint, about two-thirds of what it was, Anne tells us. The part of the store that spread to the Guthrie Centre, and the original stables area, will not be rebuilt. With seventy-five percent of Cashel Mall gone, that shrinkage isn't bad, and the store is optimistic that within three years things will be back to normal.

A huge revamp is underway in the cosmetics department, with white-tiled counters to make it look glamorously international. We are assured the store's inner core and foundation, resting on plates especially designed to move in four different ways and flex as much as a Ballantynes card, are extremely stable and could take up to a nine quake.

Meanwhile JD's Café has moved to Riccarton, there is a Ballantynes' kiosk at Merivale, and brisk business is being done online. All staff have been kept on since February and become mistresses and masters of multitasking, showing a real talent for entertaining the troops. However, there will be 'restructuring'.

After shopping there is plenty of time to wander along the gently curved main street and envy the fine old buildings, which we all imagine coming a cropper if tested by a decent-sized quake. Back in the bus, the fire services ladies wave their new bras and frocks in the air, and one of their gregarious number takes the microphone and entertains us with jokes delivered with the professional skill of a stand-up comedienne. We roar with laughter as sun pours into the left side of the bus, the snow-covered mountains pierce the heavens, and I again appreciate the raw beauty of the South Island, and the benefits of living here.

A few days later I am invited to join a local Frocks on Bikes tour, riding the circumference of the inner cordon to observe the central city before the 'dozers take it all away. The organisers call the outing 'pelotonic', as in 'Pelotonic – a ride together in a therapeutic, emotionally supportive environment whilst viewing some sad scenes'.

Life in the fridge

Frocks on Bikes was formed in Wellington in 2009 by a couple of women who turned up at a cycling event to find they were the only ones not swathed in lycra. They realised they were a breed apart and started the movement, which has since spread to other regions.

On Saturday eighteen of us turn up, including a mum, dad and nipper on a tandem, a chap on a unicycle, and a gentile noise of women on contemporary versions of sit-up-and-beg bicycles with baskets on the front. One basket has a tea towel covering muffins to distribute to security staff. We have been invited to wear black and red and have complied.

Rides take place about once a month. Apparently frocks are not essential but you get the feeling lycra would be frowned on. I am sorry to have missed the spectacle of the previous ride, which had a tweed theme. Having only just taken up cycling again in the last year (since school days), I realise the joy of cycling in a group, and, because our trusty steeds are not of the heads-down, bums-up variety, there is no need for haste and it is easy to converse.

The next day at the corner of Kilmore and Barbadoes Street I see a 'gap filler' experiment underway in the vacant lot that once housed the Herbal Dispensary. The local community has been invited to donate a book that influenced them and take one in return from an old fridge standing in the middle of the lot. I go back to the flat and rummage through the shelves, wanting to contribute and prove that life in the fridge still exists.

Stepping up to the plates

JULY 25 – It hasn't rained, it has positively poured EQC workers this week, with officials turning up at our digs to act on the second full assessment and okay the dismantling of a hard-to-budge chimney. The last mob who came through just after February 22 said they'd send the tradies around pronto to tear it down. We never saw hide nor hair of them again.

Next door, heat pumps have been installed care of EQC, over the road two houses are being bulldozed to the ground, and down the way the house that lost both its sides six months ago has at last had its flanks covered in thick black polystyrene, so great is the hustle and bustle thereof.

Kilmore Street used to throb with traffic in the old days but now, apart from the thundering of trucks and fire engines, the street is usually as quiet as a country lane. I look out the front window and am startled to observe black rabbits bunny-hopping in the grass across the road, and warn Benecio to give them and their long teeth a wide berth.

I take up an offer to accompany a pair of EQC workers to see how they operate in the field and visit a property in Strowan Road. The property looks unblemished to the untrained eye, but who knows what lies beneath that needs to be recorded and investigated?

Norm Withers (yes, the same one who kick-started the referendum on law and order) and Kirk Danger (I kid you not) – or Norm 'n' Kirk as they jokingly refer to themselves – remove their shoes at the door to show they're housetrained males and begin their inventory. They are just two of the 735 EQC workers in the field and hub, combined, in Christchurch, who start their working day at eight-thirty a.m., knock off around six, and work six days a week, with three weeks on and one week off. Norm, who has a moderate knowledge of building, works the iPad and interviews the householder – who is at the ready with proof of insurance, and the rates bill to give the size of the property. This is checked and quite often shows a discrepancy, but not in this instance.

Kirk, the builder, has, at the tender age of twenty-seven, had to quickly get his head around and grapple with going headlong into intense situations. He reflects that working for the EQC has been a huge experience. He was happily operating his own building company and living with his partner in Wellington when, back in October, he got the shoulder-tap to come down to Canterbury and lend a hand. Luckily he has a mum and siblings down here, but he flies up to Wellington late each Saturday to keep the home fires burning, returning on Sunday night.

EQC workers come from different walks of life. Norm's profile went orbital after his elderly mother was murdered in 1997 and he campaigned for tougher sentencing. He has served the city as deputy mayor, and has been working for EQC since January, when he was told the job would last two to three months max. Still it goes on.

How much the workers are paid is a sensitive issue and lips are tight, but Norm assures me the pay is more than adequate. Because workers are entering homes there is a high degree of trust involved, hence the number of former police in the ranks, and Norm stresses the need for communication, listening skills, and truckloads of patience.

Embedded in Kirk's memory is a visit to an elderly woman who lived on her own. After February 22 her home was pretty much devastated, blasted to bits. Kirk tried desperately to find the communication skills to tell her what was going on with the house. 'You have to understand that these people are just so down. I had to go outside and wonder how I could go back in and give her some good news. I find that part of the job much more of a challenge than the houses.'

Exhaustion at the end of the day is (if you'll excuse the pun) the norm, and Kirk feels lucky he has his mum to talk it through with, to put things in perspective and realise this is a once in a lifetime thing. He's seen it all, been to all points of the city, and has been here for all the big ones and on the job for most.

Most recently, on June 13, he was working down a private lane in Woolston inhabited by mostly elderly people and

Overseas journalists try to enter the inner-city cordon without appropriate accreditation. From left: Constable Scott Satherley (New Zealand Police); Senior Constable Damien Kschammer and Senior Constable Matthew Walker (South Australian Police), February 27. *Chris Hillock/The Waikato Times*

ABOVE Quinns department store in Merivale, with shoe department visible on the top floor, centre left, March 19. BELOW Mannequins in a shattered window. *Both photographs: Ross Giblin/The Dominion Post*

Oxford Terrace Baptist Church (built 1882), March 1.
Shane Cowlishaw/The Dominion Post

ABOVE Carlton Hotel (built 1906), on the corner of Papanui Road and Bealey Avenue, March 1. *Peter Drury/The Waikato Times* BELOW About a hundred people watch silently as the historic hotel is demolished, April 9. It was deemed too dangerous to be left standing. *Stacy Squires/The Press*

ABOVE Former pupils of Christchurch Girls' High School (built 1877) visit the original school building in Cranmer Square prior to its demolition, March 20. *Natasha Martin/The Timaru Herald* BELOW Demolition of shops on the corner of Bealey Avenue and Colombo Street, March 2. *Phil Reid/The Dominion Post*

Prince William attends the Christchurch earthquake memorial service in Hagley Park, March 18. On his right is the governor-general, Sir Anand Satyanand, and on his left the prime minister, John Key.
Lawrence Smith/Fairfax Media

A couple look at wreaths at the Christchurch earthquake memorial service in Hagley Park, March 18. *Lawrence Smith/Fairfax Media*

ABOVE An aerial view of liquefaction at the intersection of Maces and Ruru Roads, Bromley, after the 6.3 aftershock on June 13. *Don Scott/The Press*
BELOW Car plunged into liquefaction on Ferrymead Road following the same aftershock. *David Hallett/The Press*

single mothers when the quake struck and turned the street 'just like that, into liquefaction valley'. There was pandemonium with water cylinders, flooding, properties falling down, people screaming and panicking, and Norm and Kirk rushing five different places at once trying to calm everyone down. 'People were giving us hugs and coming back for second hugs, and then after it Norm and I actually carried on with the assessment.'

Norm says that in all the months he's been an EQC assessor he has never once had a nasty reception or struck a difficult person. 'When I ring people and say who I am and where I'm from, they've been waiting for this for a long time so it's a relief to them.' People just want to know where they are, he says, explaining that he's careful about the timing of visits. If they're running late he phones and tells the person that, because some properties take much longer than others, sorry but their house isn't going to be assessed that day.

A recipient of the Canterbury communicator of the year award, Norm is highly aware of the benefits of imparting even the smallest piece of information, because it gives people a little bit of something in the middle of a whole lot of nothing.

Kirk tells of arriving at a house and a man completely breaking down right in front of them. 'We just said, "It's all right, just let it out, it's okay." You have to have a very open mind, and be very patient. One thing I keep telling myself is to take five steps back and get an overall look at what's going on.'

Kirk goes running to relieve his stress and talks bad days through with workmates, meeting with them socially to watch a game of footy. 'That whole image of men being staunch and not talking about things has pretty much faded out.'

How long does he think he can keep working like this, I ask him, to which he replies staunchly, 'Some of us Kiwi boys in New Zealand have to step up and do it, so we're here 'til the job's done.'

Briefly Russian

AUGUST 1 – It started on Sunday. Now dirty great lumps that look like something knocked up out of polystyrene in a film studio are still loitering in the streets. This is the fag end of snow, and at the risk of sounding vulgar I guess it's what you would expect from a big dump. It terrorised the cat, who had never seen the like. He stared out the window at the white world and looked back at me as if to say, 'Do something about it.'

We'd gone out into it at four in the morning on the Monday, when it was only an inch or so deep, and as we turned to go back indoors the light of moon showed the cat's footprints next to mine in the pristine snow carpet. A pity the camera was out of action.

When the snow really piled up he refused to go out the cat door so I carried him outside to meet the call of nature. Two hours later it was getting dark and no sign of him so I started calling him, very self-conscious that 'Benecio' at the top of your voice and repeated over and over again sounds pretty pretentious. Made a mental note to call any future felines something simple and couth like Reg or Ron.

Eventually I tried next door and discovered him jammed underneath the foundations of the house, where a dog had chased him. No amount of beseeching would budge him until I removed bricks and dragged out that wuss of a puss and lugged the old boy home.

Can Christchurch ever get out of the news, what with earthquakes, heavy snowfalls and the coldest temperature since 1918? What next, people outside Canterbury, fed up with our constant domination of the news, must ask. A spot of alien invasion, perhaps? Nothing would surprise, but my god it was beautiful on Monday as three of us struck out to wander around the block observing the snowmen and trying to find somewhere open for coffee. On the corner of Armagh and Barbadoes Streets an Asian man was standing out on his third-floor balcony with his arms outstretched, beaming the biggest grin, his face registering pure delight as flakes gently drifted past him. 'Is it the first time you've seen snow?' I yelled up at him and he nodded, then shook his head, unable to believe what he was seeing.

I've seen snow, but not snow like this that doesn't disappear in a matter of hours, and I've never seen it in a city. The next day Miriam and I go to the Botanic Gardens, which are almost deserted. Hardy kids are enjoying the playground area with no waiting queues. The air is ripping with chainsaws cutting up branches that have snapped off because of the heavy freight of snow, leaving rough amputations.

There is something deeply lovely about snow meeting water. A couple of days later I get rugged and furred up and go for a punt down the Avon, feeling Dr Zhivago-esque and Russian as we glide past the glamorous white riverbanks. All that's missing are the balalaikas and huskies.

Not so glamorous is the black ice that knocks you for six, and I wait until Thursday before getting on the bike for a run to the supermarket. Even then it's a bad idea: the cars that drive too close to your flanks push you over towards the gutter, piled with hard dirty snow and slippery ice. I'm not doing another broken wrist this year.

This sort of weather calls for a good book, so I take down Paul Henry's memoir, which I have reviewed, deposit it in the fridge library, and try to find something decent in exchange. Strictly speaking, the rules of fridge library are that you have to donate a book that has had a major influence on your life and I don't think Henry's *What Was I Thinking* blew my skirt up, but I want it off my shelves. When I go back an hour later it's not there, thanks to Simon from the Garage People. He told a cobber of his I'd just taken it down and the cobber quickly rushed over and swiped it.

I look at the titles of books and don't think anyone else is playing by the rules either. There's a Barbara Taylor Bradford, a Jeffrey Archer, one history book (*The Austrian Achievement 1700–1800*), *The Television Adventures of Worzel Gummidge*, and two books that have the same name – *PS, I Love You* –

but different authors: Michael Sellers and Cecelia Ahern. The picks of the bunch are a Tim Winton and a James Ellroy, plus *The Bride Stripped Bare* by Anonymous, but I find myself drawn to the scintillatingly titled tome *Appliqué and Reverse Appliqué* and walk off with that one.

By Friday I really need some decent exercise and find myself walking deep into the heart of Linwood, where I come across the lewd spectacle of a snowman who appears to have lost his carrot nose and had it redistributed to his groin area, if snowmen have such a thing as a groin area. I stick it back in its rightful place and hear stifled laughter coming from a window and see a curtain twitch. I blush and walk briskly on, and find myself wondering if it is an offence to interfere with a snowman.

Taking care of business

AUGUST 8 – The council aims to dispense with the portaloos from our residential streets within two months. I discovered this at a workshop on how to operate compost toilets and make 'humanure' at the New Brighton community gardens on Saturday morning.

I have become quite attached to the 'turdis', as some call the portaloos. They remind me of old phone boxes and *Dr Who*. I carry the faint hope that on entering one of these tardis-like structures we may somehow be transported via a portal.

In a packed hall, the assembled, pens and paper at the ready, were told that the art to pooing and peeing in an environmentally beneficial and hygienic manner is to separate your liquids from your solids. The pee bucket is to be emptied in the morning after the first pungent pee, and the urine is to be diluted, approximately one part urine to five parts water.

When the city's pipes first took a pounding from the quakes

there were thirty-six points where raw sewage was going into the city's waterways. Now it's down to eight. However, the silt continues to challenge the pipes, causing problems with leakage, so the idea of taking care of business yourself and creating your own manure seems extremely sensible. All you need is two buckets, a box structure with a loo lid, and a wheelie bin into which to transfer the excrement. The deposits should be layered with brown organic matter – to break it down before it can be distributed on the garden.

We were told that if anyone in the household is involved with the partaking of drugs, either of the recreational or prescription varieties, their waste products weren't welcome as they would have sinister effects on the vegetable patch. It immediately sprang to mind that this scenario might be responsible for the sexist expression 'mad woman's excrement'.

The chap giving the demonstration was loath to use the word 'waste' when referring to dung. It implied that human excrement was a dirty business, when in fact, if nasty chemicals were kept out of the picture, our poo was hot stuff environmentally.

Apparently if you have a reticulated system outside the front gate you are legally required to be connected to it, but that doesn't mean you have to *use* your flushing toilet. Looking round the two hundred or so crowd I wondered how many were there to swap over to a compost toilet for good, had (or still have) to use one because of the quakes, were good scouts and being prepared in the event of another biggie, or were survivalists.

Whoever they were, they were an inquiring bunch, and hardly a step along the process was allowed to continue without a hand shooting up with a question about what was allowed in the mix and what wasn't. Vomit and diarrhea, vinegar, toilet paper and food scraps were all admissible, but chemicals and tampons weren't. A woman volunteered the information that moon cups were preferable to sanitary napkins and that a workshop on how to use such a thing was in the pipeline, as it were.

Somebody wanted to know if meat eaters should be using the same bucket as vegetarians. Another suggested that worms could be added to the mix. When we were told handfuls of soil could be used to help the process of breakdown, a New Brighton resident said there wasn't much of that stuff left in Brighton, to which the speaker advised stocking up whenever visiting the other side of town. It was only afterwards it occurred to me that I had failed to ask whether females on oral contraception were banned from the communal organic throne to prevent hormones entering the food chain and causing D cups, as opposed to moon ones, in gents.

It took a good two hours for the compost information to be divulged, and if the plumbing goes to pack this system seems a whole lot easier and cleaner than digging a hole in the garden. Apparently the abiding memory of the American forces who served in Korea was the stench of human excrement *sans* composting spread raw over the fields, whereas in this process the excrement takes nine months to break down and becomes odour-free and hygienically sorted.

Later in the day I attended the Hiroshima commemoration ceremony, held since the mid '70s in Victoria Square, where the lanterns were lit and floated down the river. With the square now in the Red Zone, the organisers had attempted to relocate the ceremony to the Peace Bell in the Botanic Gardens, but alas that too had been red-stickered so it was held at the WEA.

Over a hundred people turned up. A Japanese choir and the granddaughter of Elsie Locke sang. The daughter of Japanese anti-nuclear activists who immigrated to New Zealand twenty years ago announced that since the Fukushima disaster Japan has decided that having nuclear reactors in an earthquake-prone country isn't such a good idea: all fifty-four are to be shut down.

That night I walk with a neighbour over to a bowling green in Gracefield Avenue to listen to five bands perform. It seems an impossible ask for tipsy patrons to keep off the grass but the rule is adhered to and a good time had by all. Walking both there and back we appear to be the only foot traffic on the street, and only five cars pass us by.

Where is everybody? They can't all be at home watching the rugger. I keep expecting to see Bruno Lawrence walk into the picture to add perspective to the quiet earth.

The all shook up future

AUGUST 15 – Mayor Bob Parker has asked the people of Christchurch to be big-hearted and -minded and embrace the draft plan. The city gingerly sniffs it, deciding if this vision of the future is up to everybody's scratch.

Prime minister John Key's low-key reaction reiterates his girthquake-recovery minister's statement that it's 'a very big wish list'. This indicates a tight-wad post-election government spend on the city's rebirth.

The draft – drawn from 106,000 submissions and with more wishes than a Santa sack – is critical to the city's psyche as it tries to right itself, like a foal standing up on ice. The June 13 aftershocks put the frighteners on the reinsurers. Residents in the red cashed up, but with no real confidence to gamble it all on building anew without an insurance safety net, nor to stay in a city which has had no vision for a very long time as the mayor and council have done their best to create the perception of inclusiveness to every idea in order to carry the people with them.

The announcement of the draft plan provides badly needed direction and some hope to those who have been scrabbling round blindly in the gloom of constant destruction, waiting for a purchase on a future.

After the February devastation of the CBD, the repeated mantra that we have only one chance to get it right has put immense pressure on tomorrow's city – and a drastic change in the mindset of a place that has had so much of its identity tied up in heritage.

The proposed seven-storey height limit for new buildings in the CBD has already produced misgivings in the real estate industry that owners of multistorey buildings will be short-changed by not being able to replicate their buildings to their former height and, with less rental space, will lose money. Others say the reduced skyline will fail to look like an international city, even though there are some tall buildings still standing, which could stick out like the proverbial sore thumb in the new cool urban design. But consideration had to be given to those trapped and traumatised in high-rises during the quakes, and these people will no doubt think even seven storeys is too high. But if the central business district is to be smaller, that has to be a consideration too.

A year ago the retail heart of the city was, if you will excuse the pun, no great shakes. It was overrun with bland generic outlets drearily repeated in every town and city nationally and internationally. Why make the effort to journey to the centre for the same old same old, when you can get it in a mall close to home? For all his failings, the property developer Dave Henderson looked at the south of the city, with its curiosity of alleyways and quaint dwellings, and turned it into a lively alternative to the strip malls. Unfortunately the area was a casualty of the quakes and has gone forever, but it is hoped that 'the new' doesn't prohibit the bohemian flavour once sought out and celebrated in Christchurch's streets.

Already, commerce is threatening not to buy into the CBD low-rise plan, and the fear is that businesses will do what they have been doing since February: grow like Topsy in an ad hoc manner. It would be a terrible disappointment if the city failed to replace its heart and lurched elsewhere. We desperately need a real city so we can say farewell to the soulless days of working in pods, hubs and pop-ups.

Entrepreneurs with the will and guts to come back to the centre should be mindful of creating shopping clusters that are excitably different. Stores with high cultural value – such as Scorpio books, which has resettled in Riccarton Road – may never feel the need to return to the heart. However, those who scattered to residential zones and want to stay there are on a time limit of five years, before the slack the council has cut them drives them reluctantly back into the city. Hopefully, the carrots offered to move them back in under one umbrella will be enough of an incentive.

The proposal for a 406-million-dollar light rail network is laudable with the petrol crisis and the post-quake fear of multi-level car parks, but the plan for a rail route between central Christchurch and Canterbury University is a risk. Research about where students are living after the quake needs to be done before that is made the first imperative.

Then there is the eight million dollars being set aside for a memorial. There is no doubt in any Cantabrian mind that some kind of memorial is needed to acknowledge the loss of life, and the psychic pain that continues to take its toll after the tragedy. Launching the draft plan, Parker movingly dedicated it 'to the people we've lost', but having a costly mausoleum to the dead does not bring them back, nor help the living move on. The national memorial service held al fresco in Hagley Park on March 11 showed we do not need a grand building to meaningfully come together and commemorate the dead. Announcing a grandiose plan is a huge expectation-raiser, and carries the risk it may be used as a lambasting rod to cane genuine efforts to create something truly special. Surely it would be more profound to acknowledge those who perished with a series of appropriate installations along the riverside in the proposed, widened Avon River Park, possibly manifesting in lights a dedication to each of them? That way their deaths would be kept as part of the continuum.

On Sunday snow returns to the city, with forecasts saying it will be with us for the week. My brother, the vicar, has returned from England and is living with me until he finds new digs. Benecio doesn't think much of his dog collar and by Monday, with the snow heavy on the ground, we realise we will be living cheek-by-jowl, getting under each other's feet and paws as we navigate the igloo and cope with cabin fever.

This has been the longest year I can remember and there's still plenty more of it to come with the Rugby World Cup and the elections. Old Bucky is still here, his cogitations registering in the background as he keeps his hand in, delivering small belts around the twos. We still make sure to touch wood as we dare to say out loud, 'I haven't felt any aftershocks lately.'

I remove from the front door the green city council sticker I was so relieved to slap up way back in February as proof of valid occupancy, and file it away for posterity in the camphor box. I imagine somebody rummaging through the box in years to come and looking at the sticker will wonder why the old lady bothered to keep that.

Snow falling on ruins

AUGUST 22 – A series of small ailments has mocked the immune system, then a two-day flu wormed its way in past the defences and I took to the couch, nursing a dodgy chest that felt as if a host of martial arts instructors had practised their kick-boxing upon it. Friends rang and delivered right tellings-off for the foolhardiness of not having a flu injection as I uttered mea culpas and waited for the pathogens to slope off.

Our shrunken world in Christchurch got even smaller with our second bout of snow. The city's streets showed how disenchanted they were this time round with only a limited turnout of snowmen – or snowpersons if I am to be politically correct. According to the publican down the road, 'There's no man like a snowman'. Everyone texted each other, relieved at signs our local watering hole was going to reopen, as delivery trucks heroically managed to get through.

Snow falling on ruins

My brother returned from overseas and camped out at my digs, staring out the front window judging weather conditions before dashing out at regular intervals to shovel madly away at the drive and the front steps, and run the car up and down the driveway to get a groove going.

The large front window became like a giant TV screen showing only one channel. We watched cars skidding down the road to come to grief in moguls, and wiled away the claustrophobic hours trying to come up with book titles with the word 'snow' in them – such as *Snow Falling on Cedars* and *Miss Smilla's Feeling for Snow* – and rummaged around in the CD collection trying to locate *The White Album*, or a bit of Bing dreaming of his white Christmas.

It feels as though the gods of boredom are taunting us with more of plenty of nothing, on top of the city's chronic lack of venues, as the weather insists on being inclement and shutting us down. If only the video collection had been liberated from that church of culture and escapism Alice in Videoland, we would be taking our confinement to barracks a whole lot better. Surely the council or CERA or someone can see the good sense in getting the guts out of Alice's and relocating them somewhere else?

At least Old Bucky seemed to be in a pattern of retreat. I imagined the collision of ground frozen with a seal of black ice and rising liquefaction should a sizeable quake hit. When the four-pointer came early on Saturday morning, it shook the house so badly it felt like the proverbial pack of cards. As the rumble seemed to continue for an age, I felt duty-bound to go out to the sitting room, where I observed a guest, deep in sleep and well versed in shakes, expertly roll off the couch in her sleeping bag to lie beside it in case the roof fell in.

You could forgive us for thinking we're living in Old Testament times with quakes, unprecedented bouts of snow, and Ice Age temperatures. I neurotically find myself wondering what the natural world has in store for us next – perhaps a visitation of locusts, a deluge of frogs, or a plague of boils?

When the snow recedes, leaving mounds that look like dirty lemonade, I wander down to the café and can't believe my eyes when I see what appears to be Benecio Lite wandering across my path. I pick up the beast and see the only thing that stops her from being the lad's twin is her diminutive size and the absence of a Heidelberg duelling scar across one eye. I discover she lives down the road and her name is Aphrodite, Aphro for short, and she has a reputation for wandering into strange houses and spending the night. Perhaps she could wander down and spend the night with Benecio and they could furtively make beautiful music together, although it might be many a moon since the old boy registered a barbarous stirring in the trouser department.

On the way back I call in to see the Garage People and make admiring noises to Simon about the conversion of an old television cabinet on castor wheels into a three-element gas burner. He's been toiling at it endlessly so it can be pushed out of the garage swiftly if 'the big 'un happens'. Talk about being prepared. You should see the mountain of toilet paper stockpiled from floor to ceiling in the bathroom as this mature boy scout embraces the 'Be prepared' motto and entertains end-of-world fantasies.

The cabinet is painted what my mother used to call menopausal blue and stands proudly at the front of the garage. With a series of round holes cut in the top to let the vapours through, it would stump many an observer as to its use. I tell the artist it could be discovered and appear on *Antiques Roadshow* in 2030, should the world still be spinning in that distant future. There is no name for such an original creation, but to me it looks like the sort of thing an extraterrestrial might use for a drinks cabinet.

Learning to swim

AUGUST 29 – Not wanting to feel left out after the snow, Jack Frost has been making his presence felt keenly in the early morning, while the weather in the middle part of the day has been absolutely top shelf. Girls keen to show off their latest tattoos can be seen wandering the streets in skimpy summer frocks, their bare arms and legs turning nipple pink as they work on an early tan. At this rate we'll be fishing around in the bottom drawer to break out the togs, the only small problem being where to swim.

In the olden days inner-city residents could stroll down to the Centennial Pool to enjoy its two pools and wet and dry saunas, and watch yelping small fry learn the life-saving water skills of how to keep afloat. The Centennial Pool was an oasis of activity year-round, and of all the facilities, apart from the central library, it is missed the most.

The draft plan talks of an aquatic centre containing an

Learning to swim

Olympic-sized swimming pool to be built around the Red Bus and AMI Stadium area, but it won't be up and ready for six years. With so many school pools damaged or beyond repair, the Centennial pronounced a goner, and the QEII Sport Centre out of action, that is far too late for a generation of Christchurch children; in the near future they may contribute to the Water Safety Council statistic that each year in New Zealand an average of twenty children under the age of fifteen drown.

There is something un-New-Zealand about children at knee-high-to-a-grasshopper stage not being able to learn to swim. One can imagine Christchurch teenagers of the future sitting it out on sandy sidelines at beaches, miserably watching their peers frolicking in the waves and having to explain they never learnt to swim because of the earthquakes. What is to be done? Perhaps other places rich in aquatic centres could arrange for Christchurch kids to attend swim camps.

The actual state of damage to the Centennial Pool remains a mystery and people, especially those with young families, want to know why it can't be repaired. Does its close proximity to the river put it in the required thirty-metre building-free set-back from the Avon? Is building or repairing any facility on indefinite hold while insurance and reinsurance companies wait for the shaking to stop?

The draft plans have made us aware of statistics that we didn't know previously. For example, before the February quake I didn't know that those of us living centrally numbered approximately 8,000, and that there were predicted to be

30,000 inner-city residents within the four avenues by the year 2016. It seems hard to envisage that as I look across the street to bowled-over sections, and a bulldozer's claw lying spent beside a garage that has a 'Do not demolish sign' slapped across its sides and front. The new build in the residential inner city can go up to 14 metres with no buffering. If this goes ahead it will be a radical change to our mostly one- and two-storey old houses and art deco apartments.

There is no official figure for those who have fled or given up and quit the core, but those left have become the usual suspects in a ragbag line-up of owners and renters. With so much talk of girthquake, some worry we are going to become the poster boys and girls of obesity tourism so we go for calorie-consuming walks in the neighbourhood. It is heartbreaking to see spring flowers coming through in the gardens of abandoned houses whose owners have laboured over the planting of daphne bushes, violets, japonica and daffodils. Now there is no one to pick the flowers and put them in vases.

You can imagine the displaced watching the calendar and wondering wistfully how the lemon tree is doing this year after the snows. I can report that the answer is extremely well. Trees groan with lemons and the big yellow fruit scatter on the ground. It makes you want to lift the latch of the gate, briskly walk in and scoop up a handful because it looks as if no one's coming back to get them. However, the thought of appearing in front of an old beak on a charge of lemon-looting kills the base impulse.

Like the Australian city of Darwin, which experiences a build-up before the rains, there is an emotional build-up going on in Christchurch as we hurtle towards the anniversary of the first quake. The city, what's left of it, will be descended upon by swarms of media. A searchlight of hope is to shine from the top of a Cathedral Square building until February 22 and we will try and arrange our fragile faces and hold hands round the Red Zone.

A couple of days ago I walked as far as you can to the end of Chester Street East at the edge of the zone and inched along a gap between the wire cordon and the neighbouring fence line. The builders' constant friend, the commercial radio station, was turned up full blast. The Oasis Hotel, where I sometimes dined with the Aged Parents, has been totally gutted and there appeared to be no activity going on in any building from there to Latimer Square. A man in hard hat and fluoro jacket appeared around the corner and started to furiously sweep up a mound of rubble among an impossibility of rubble. It seemed to represent the enormity of the situation.

Our own 9/4

SEPTEMBER 5 – In the past week I kept hearing people describe yesterday's special date as the September 4 'celebrations', while others called it an 'anniversary' or a 'commemoration'. None of these words seems to fit the passing of a year since Old Bucky first cleared his throat and gave us a 7.1 kick, starting over 7,000 aftershocks. If you can't live with the earthquakes you move away from them, people advise, to which my reaction is: Where can you smugly hang your hat and feel safe these dodgy days, now we know in a very real sense what it's like to live in the Shaky Isles?

In the last year I've travelled out of Christchurch only twice – once for a fleeting visit to Auckland a month after February 22, and last week to Wellington to work. I lie, I also went on a bus trip to Ballantynes in Timaru, but there was no sleepover so that doesn't count. Normally I travel much more but I got it into my head that as I was tasked with writing about the quake I had a responsibility to be here, to use a hackneyed term, 24/7. What if another big one hit and I had swanned off elsewhere? I'd look a fraud, wouldn't I?

In Wellington I started to fret about not having time to get around and see all my old cobbers, who would be as cross as two sticks if they heard I was in town and hadn't visited or arranged to meet. Talk about winding yourself up unnecessarily. On Thursday night I stayed at a friend's place in Brooklyn, and on Friday morning the friend was on the computer in my bedroom reading the Stuff website. When I nipped out to have a shower she removed the story about the 4.9 earthquake that had happened in my absence because she thought it would worry me. In the meantime another well-meaning friend rang up and left a message on the cellphone that I wasn't to worry about the 4.9 that had just hit Christchurch. I must have the word 'neurotic' tattooed across my forehead.

I had accepted an invitation to appear on a panel discussion about crisis communications from the perspective of someone living in the inner city. The event was held in a hotel in Cuba Street. When I lived in Wellington I used to walk down Cuba Street pretty much every day and took the bohemian cross-cultural atmosphere for granted. I don't know if everyone's moved to Wellington post quake but Cuba Mall was teeming with even more people, particularly young groovers in their twenties. Overwhelmed at the sight of so many humans, I retreated back to the hotel and found a quiet corner next to a baby grand that was playing computerised music to itself, an invisible player liberally applying soft peddle while belting out the Mozart.

Wellington seems to have become a mecca for young people, a startling contrast to Christchurch, which is dominated by a middle-aged to old-aged population. Many people have talked about the need for fresh young blood to come to Christchurch for the rebuild, but at the moment a venue-less city isn't a good place in which to meet and mate. Perhaps it could take a leaf out of Invercargill mayor Tim Shadbolt's book and offer budget university education as an enticement.

The next day I met a friend in a restaurant on the corner of Kent Terrace and Majoribanks Street and found myself feeling quite queasy and lizard-eyed, hyper-aware of the traffic at the busy intersection and the thick streams of people jostling the footpaths. Good grief, get a grip girl, I thought, realising how small-town and narrow-minded I must have become from living in a reduced, shrunk-down world. There's certainly plenty of frenetic activity to be had in the 'burbs of Christchurch but the inner city is so quiet they could sell tickets to it as a meditation retreat.

I like quiet. I like the melancholy of a deserted street. I love going to movies in the afternoon when there are only two people in the theatre. I am irritated by crowded, loud, crash-bang restaurants and cafes. I loathe queues. I strongly suspect I have become a card-carrying, twenty-four-carat femudgeon: a female curmudgeon. I visit my old house in Mount Cook. The guy who lives there now makes me a cup of tea and kindly lets me sit up the back of the garden for a quiet moment.

    Back at home the big news on the street is that in a few days Kilmore Street is going to open up all the way to Manchester Street. I text the news to the neighbours; we are all excited that our world is inching bigger. The huge white arch stretching from one side of Kilmore Street to the other, erected to temporarily house the fire trucks, will be dismantled and we can again cross what we used to call as children the Billy Goat Gruff Bridge. Along with the white arch I wish they'd get rid of that rusty tribute to 9/11. We have our own 9/4 to be getting on with.

Mall life

SEPTEMBER 12 – I am walking home after dark, traipsing behind a couple of youths, when one of them points to the skies and asks what the White Lights of Hope are. His mate snorts derisively. 'Where've you been? That's Jason Gunn's wife's thingies.'

I like the White Lights of Hope because they remind me of the lights that used to pierce the night sky during the Industries Fair. Others say they make the place look even more like a World War II bombsite or POW camp than it does already. Perhaps we could build on that theme and employ street performers, kitting them out in Colonel Klink, Colonel Hogan and Sergeant Shultz costumes and having them give chase around the cordon. Every time something greater than a five-point aftershock hits, an air-raid siren could be set off to join the cacophony of sirens heard every day in the inner city.

Mall life

Now that our street has opened up down to Manchester Street, I've been taking advantage of the new route and have become more aware of the hookers. According to the paper, most have packed up their thigh-length boots and gone up north for a while to Auckland's rich pickings during the Rugby World Cup. On Thursday morning I ventured out for an early morning blat on the bike and observed a grand total of two ladies of the night standing on the corner of Bealey Avenue and Manchester Street in almost broad daylight, sporting red and black garb in Canterbury colours in a show of loyalty to the province.

The prostitutes aren't the only defectors to Auckland. A few weeks back I foolishly agreed to participate in a chefs vs. food critics night at something called Taste Events, and on Sunday the evil day had come around. I was disturbed to discover that we were expected to spend the entire afternoon slaving away preparing the dishes, before plating up for eighty punters that evening. Why do we say yes to these things? Needless to say the critics lost – especially as the team was hampered by a TV reviewer who wouldn't know her angel hair pasta from her elbow. Anyway, when everyone had their noses in the food I got talking to the chefs, who said you can't get a junior chef in this town for love or money. There are plenty of kitchen hands and waiters but Auckland has poached all the middle ranks, leaving the major domos to battle on alone at the helm of the few kitchens still operating.

The east has been without The Palms mall – or The Sweaty Palms, as a relative calls it – since February 22, but it reopened on Thursday morning at nine and I trooped along to see the fanfare. A piper had been positioned down at the far end, next to a tent set up to screen the rugby, and a clown had his work cut out for him twisting balloons into the usual shapes for a small crowd, a high percentage of whom seemed to be suffering from coulrophobia, a fear of clowns.

The Aussie owner of The Palms, who has silver bodgie hair in the manner of Bob Hawke, had flown across the Tasman for the occasion. As exhausted hard-hatted construction teams and engineers looked on proudly he said it was the first time in forty-five years his company had had to close a centre. Shopkeepers all said the same thing – 'You should have seen the place yesterday' – and talked about the mad panic to be ready for opening day, but all were happy to be back at work after six months' enforced sabbatical.

In the old days you would have been hard-pressed to find a space in the car park but there were plenty to be had on Thursday morning. Perhaps shoppers don't want to risk being sandwiched and squashed in another quake, although every single column in the car park and building has been stripped back to check for damage, and restrengthened with high-strength concrete and a carbon fibre wrapping. Eighty shops are back in business, with Kmart, Farmers and Reading Cinemas opening later in the year, and the mall sports new flooring; 300 tiles were replaced and the whole floor regrouted after liquefaction pierced the surface.

I wandered into a hairdressing joint and was the first customer to get a wash and blow-dry as the staff rushed round trying to locate their equipment in the refitted shop, which is still waiting on carpet and wallpaper. About two hours later I emerged, blinking myopically, into natural light and remembered why I don't miss mall life.

Two months ago there was a piece on TV3's *Campbell Live* about rumours the Riccarton mall wasn't safe. A couple of aggrieved nannies re-enacted phone conversations with each other, nasally voicing their worries about the state of the mall and the car park – from which, wild rumour had it, someone had removed the red sticker.

The mall, the nannies said, was their home. They went there every day with their charges. I hoped their employers were watching and hopping mad to discover they were paying for their small fry to spend most of their days like battery hens, cavorting under artificial light in the mall's playground as the nannies gossiped and sipped lattes from the sidelines.

The malls have also become mating grounds for teenagers, who congregate there in droves, the rash of their troubled skin on harsh display in the unforgiving lighting. Give me the soft crepuscular gloom of the back of the bike sheds any day, rather than piped music, whopping great TVs screening reruns of great sporting moments and writhing music videos, generic shops, and travelators to wither away the calf muscles. With so many unnatural distractions and nasty lighting it is a wonder anyone can summon up the strength to mate.

Funkytown museum

SEPTEMBER 19 – The taxi driver I selected from the Auckland airport cab rank asked me where I'd come from and when I said Christchurch he raised his left hand off the wheel, shook it in an imitation of a tremble, and asked, 'So how is Shaky Town?' His nickname for our city has left me with the brain worm 'Won't you take me to funkytown?', which I can't seem to dislodge from my inner soundtrack.

A friend suggested we take a visit to the new Auckland art gallery and I found myself being driven through downtown Auckland, leaning forward to get a better look and perving up like a country hick at modern highrise buildings with wonderment and awe.

When I got back home, I woke up in the middle of the night to the bed shaking and thought it was an aftershock but it was only Benecio giving himself a comprehensive wash, licking himself to death in his own mobile dry-cleaning unit.

'Imagine if we humans carried on like that,' I said to him, forming a mental image of licking the back of my hand and swiping it over the back of an ear.

Next morning I took a wander down Barbadoes Street and passed one of the many middle-aged to elderly male eccentrics who dwell in the inner city and seem to spend most of their days walking the streets. A bulldozer was dismantling a couple of old weatherboard shacks and there was a miserable pile of abandoned belongings, including a couple of kapok mattresses that looked as though they dated back to the Crimean War.

The old guy, who was muttering away to himself, came right up to me and shouted in my face, 'Nothing left soon, nothing left!'

'Quite,' I said, wiping the spit off my cheek.

I went home, ploughed through a mound of piled-up newspapers and discovered, joy of joys, the museum had reopened. Nothing for it then but to pick up a cobber who said he wouldn't mind saying gidday to the place, and after a couple of laps of the Brian Brake and Peter Bush photographs there we were, taking a nostalgic stroll down the old 'Christchurch Street' to make sure the horse was still there. Having just dismounted from the penny-farthing bike, I was emboldened to put my foot in the stirrup and hoist myself up, but a spoilsport notice next to the old nag said only people aged thirteen and under were allowed a go.

We discovered a multi-storey Dunedin doll's house in the tiny Ballantynes store, and on closer inspection the interior, especially the lower floors, appeared to be in disarray. Chairs and lamps were on the ground, a grandfather clock had hit the deck, the paintings on the wall were askew, crockery and books were in a jumble – it looked like there'd been a bloody earthquake. There had. A notice explained that after February 22 the staff had found the exhibit in this state and, on reflection, decided to leave it 'as is' to demonstrate the chaos in the microcosm. All that was missing were a couple of miniature EQC guys knocking on the front door.

When I was a kid everyone at Rangiora Borough School was granted a trip to the museum and some luckier ones got to travel on the ferry up to Wellington to visit parliament. I remember, during the first museum visit, coming around a corner and seeing the big globe of the world doing a spin, and being able to stand underneath it on the sunken floor and mount the stairs to view the top of the world from a platform. It was dead exciting, widely considered to be the bee's knees, and there it still is today, looking a bit shabbier and smaller, but then it would wouldn't it, after all that's happened.

On the way home we stopped off for just the one at the black makeshift bar where the Carlton Hotel used to be. A path of green AstroTurf wended through what appeared to be a giant tray of kitty litter as we made our way to the bar and ordered a couple of glasses of their best house sauvignon blanc. The boy barman retrieved a wine bottle with about an inch left in it from the fridge and tossed it in a showy flip in the air before it landed back in his hand. My memory of the film *Cocktail* is sketchy but I'm sure Tom Cruise flipped only top-shelf bottles and I was worried the boy had bruised our grapes.

Sitting al fresco in a sea of kitty litter on indoors padded furniture with a view out on to the traffic of Papanui Road left us feeling more than a little unhinged. Later on I biked past the Copthorne Hotel and saw a crane standing by with a skip swinging from it. A worker in a hotel room with broken windows was wearily clearing out the room, chucking the contents into the skip. On the ground a whole line of skips, full to the gunnels, waited to be taken off to a dump. I remembered the old man's words: 'Nothing left soon, nothing left.'

In the spirit

SEPTEMBER 26 – Now that the fire trucks are safely tucked up in their beds, rather than spending their nights out under a temporary awning in the middle of the road, you might have thought Kilmore Street would once again throb with traffic. Not so, which is a blessing. The only noise on the street you hear out of school hours is the gentle thud of boys gripped by Rugby World Cup fever kicking footballs back and forth, aping the great Dan Carter.

On Tuesday I dropped into the fan zone in Hagley Park to see what was on offer under the mysterious white tents. The place was pretty much people- and fun-free. A handful of women were sitting in a tent trying to flog off rugby jerseys and paraphernalia and they confessed takers had been few on the ground. A couple of stands and a miniature goalpost deserted of movement added to the eerie atmosphere, but there was a tiny frenzy of activity down in the Science Alive tent, where ankle-biters were joyfully hurling footballs at a net in an unscientific manner.

Security guards and officials were tripping over themselves as I approached the inflatable dome that is the World Ruck nostalgia zone. A woman and a boy were parked up on a couch in the noughties' zone, desultorily watching a recent All Blacks' test. Feeling like a freshly appointed tsar, I realised I had dominion over and free range of all the other zones painstakingly created by CPTI (Christchurch Polytechnic Institute of Technology) students.

The nostalgia lounges were furnished with Formica for the '50s, a cocktail set for the '60s, a beanbag and nasty wallpaper for the '70s, and I must admit I nearly shed a tear to happen upon an old Philips TV set in the '80s zone. My god they made good sets back then, built to last and capable of standing to attention through the most brutal earthquakes. And they had decent sound systems too, not like these pansy flat-screen numbers you have to put up with today, all picture and shoddy sound that has to be fed through a stereo to get any decent level of grunt.

The least I could do, I thought, feeling as if all this had been laid on for me, would be to buy a cup of coffee so I placed my order with a barista, who nearly fainted with excitement to be doing business. There's only so much fun a girl can have so I then untied the blue pony from the bike stand, where it had been the only horse in a one-horse town, and peddled across the paddock, feeling a little like Bruno Lawrence must have felt in *The Quiet Earth*.

In the weekend I drove out to Addington Raceway to have a gander at the Body Mind Spirit Festival. It was five bucks to get in and the place heaved with alternatives pushing crystals, spiritual healing with laying-on of hands, and card and palm readings. There was even a stall where people had their feet deeply immersed in what looked like fresh cow manure.

Bugger the expense, I found myself forking out fifteen dollars to lie down on a plank for fifteen minutes while a woman made me drape my arm in the manner of Kenneth Williams as she tapped my paw and instructed my body to strengthen itself and remove any blockages. At one stage I had to lift up a leg and bend it in the air while she assured me no one was looking up my dress. A passerby stopped to have a gawk.

Another woman with a pack of fairy and angel cards told me prosperity was on its way, as she kept up a commentary with the spirit guides and ate chocolates. Had anything she'd said made a connection, she asked. It hadn't, but not wishing to spoil her fun I eventually obliged by nodding and giving her what I thought might pass for a beatific soulful smile.

Another chap was conducting breathing tests and, as I often find myself not breathing, I submitted to holding my breath as he encouraged me on, registering the seconds on a stopwatch while I turned puce in the face. Apparently I had scored the best in show of the day, but alas I was still breathing well below capacity. There's no pleasing some people

While I was in that neck of the woods I thought I'd drop into the CBS Arena for a snack and wondered why the table of men opposite me in the café were sporting heavy maquillage and wearing what looked like hired suits. The penny dropped when women swathed in satin dressing gowns with sequins in their hair teetered past to buy lunch: they were taking a break from the national and international ballroom dancing competitions. I thought about hanging around until the action started up again, but remembered as a small child going to a ballroom dancing competition, being impaled by a stiletto, and having my cheeks grazed as I copped a face full of net when a competitor drifted badly off course in the two-step.

The peppy aftershocks during the week seem to have brought with them a cat that meows piteously as Benecio stares at him contemptuously through the glass of the cat door. I give the stray a couple of days' feed close to the gate so he won't get the wrong idea about moving in but enough so he can find his way home again. Benecio catches me at it and looks at me with deep loathing. I look at the cat door and, inspired by Body Mind Spirit, imagine setting up rebirthing courses for rich cats as they step through the flap into enlightenment. I think the idea has legs.

Marching orders

OCTOBER 3 – The earthquakes have laid waste to galaxies of movie theatres so in the last year I've seen only two films. One was the documentary *Sam Hunt – Purple Balloon and Other Stories* out at the quaint Hollywood Theatre in Sumner; the other was *Jane Eyre*, screening at a movie theatre I daren't mention for fear of getting the ticket issuer into trouble.

It was a beautiful day, the sun was pouring down like honey, so I got in the car and drove to the mall. I noted how dimly lit the movie theatre stairs were as I stumbled forth in the sepulchral gloom towards the ticket counter.

'One ticket please to *Jane Eyre*,' I asked, inwardly congratulating myself for having the willpower to refrain from requesting a chocolate-covered ice cream as well.

To my horror the guy behind the ticket counter replied, 'I don't mean you to read anything into this but I'll do you a favour and put you through as a senior citizen.'

Marching orders

Feeling a day older than God I reached out to get the change, and with ten minutes to wait sat down feebly on a chair in the vestibule and scratched round in my reticule, looking for the magazine I'd brought with me to peruse if there was a wait. Unfortunately the lighting was too dim to read anything with my $2 Shop glasses, of which I have several pairs stationed around the flat (we oldies are so forgetful about where we leave them) so I gave up and went into the dark of the theatre and waited and waited and waited.

After some considerable time a trailer for a film began, then just as quickly as it had appeared the visual disappeared, leaving us with only the soundtrack. Because it was a late-morning screening there was only a handful of us in the theatre, but, already well on the way to being a curmudgeon, I thought: Some other muggins can go and find out what's happening.

A semi-deserted movie theatre has its advantages because if someone's talking around you or unwrapping noisy sweets you can move away, but when something goes wrong with the film or sound you feel as if you are on an abandoned spaceship. Eventually a woman got up out of her seat and shuffled off, returning a while later to relay the information that 'He's having trouble with the projector.'

I'm this side of fifty but the ticket-holder had ignited my paranoia: I wished I'd asked him to put me through as a student or a child. I started counting up how many versions of *Jane Eyre* I'd seen, estimating it at five. I must be bloody ancient to have seen five *Jane Eyre*s I thought, as I tried to get into the latest one unfolding in front of me.

Just the other day a friend was commenting how sick she was of looking at demolition and added, 'I guess we will become just as tired of reconstruction, when and if it happens.' We were a few minutes into *Jane Eyre* and I was adjusting to Mr Rochester's northern accent, when what sounded like a loud pneumatic drill started up in close proximity. As it kept happening, completely destroying any transport into gothic fiction, once I'd observed Mr Rochester propose to Jane and kiss her with unconvincing passion I got up and walked out.

I didn't have the concentration or courage to witness what was ahead: Mr Mason interrupting the nuptial ceremony, Jane fleeing her soulmate and decamping into the miserable moors, the house burning down, Mr Rochester's face getting badly burnt and scarred. I didn't want to see the wholesale emotional demolition of it all.

I'd been home only a short while when there was a knock on the door and Lorraine was standing there telling me the Garage People had been given their marching orders, three months' notice, and were on the move. As Tui, who used to work at the corner hairdresser's shop and was a habitué of the garage, explained it, 'The Garage People are great because they keep the vibe of the street going.'

Like every other person in their twenties, Tui's gone to Australia to try her luck and now the Garage People are leaving the street too. Their garage has become an unofficial drop-in community centre where you can draw up a pew and chew the fat, crake a quake chat, and have a laugh. It will be sad to see the door drawn down and not have Simon yell out as I bike past, 'Your wheels are going forward, Lady Jane.'

A few days later Lorraine tells me they've found another flat just round the corner and Simon's borrowed the shopping trolley belonging to Penguin, who does the circular deliveries, and is gradually moving their belongings to the new digs. It's the end of an era, but as my Dad would often say at the bottom of a glass of wine, 'All good things must come to an end.' And I would pipe back, 'Why?'

It was a fine warm day on Saturday for a 'red-stickered-be-damned jam' party on a hillside property. I've missed the view of the mountains I took for granted at my parents' place in Mount Pleasant and felt strangely moved to be standing on the verandah and looking across at the good old alps. Peering down into the properties below, I could see where large boulders had come to a frightening full stop in backyards. Meanwhile, in the living room the band rocked on. What strange times we live in.

Love and loathing in the dunes

OCTOBER 10 – September 28 has long come and gone, and the leaflet published by an alarmist North Canterbury fundamentalist Christian who did a Martin Luther King, as in had a dream, predicting massive earthquake and floods still loiters about the mess of my desk.

On the day of the prediction I drove out to Woodend Beach, which was to receive a tsunami that would destroy the camping ground lodge before continuing to the south skirts of Tuahiwi. When I was growing up on the Canterbury Plains, hills were something of a novelty. As I parked my car in the empty car park I noticed with amazement how small the sand dune was at the entrance to the beach. When I was a child that hill seemed insurmountably Egmontian, a necessary evil to sweat and climb over in the blaze of summer to get to the cool of the waves and the expanse of the beach.

I remember asking my father how the border for each

beach was decided – when did Woodend become Waikuku, Pines or Leithfield? – and thinking that, with so much beach to see clear up to Brighton and just as far the other way, nobody would mind or even notice if we took a chunk of it back home with us to inland Rangiora.

In my teens I managed to convince my strict parents to let me go on a Christian youth camp holiday at Woodend. This was in the days when fundamentalists and evangelicals were first making their presence felt in our small town, which was already heaving with odd religions. On Friday nights the girls would wear bum-freezer (as my mother called them) miniskirts and parade up and down the main street, while the lads would cruise past in their Mark II Zephyrs attempting to entice the girls in and drive them down to Groynes Reserve or the banks of the Ashley, where, after sips of Blackberry Nip, they would repair to the back seat.

If you weren't trying to avoid teenage pregnancy you were trying to keep out of the clutches of the Cooperites, who set up vantage points on the main drag and tried to lure the young and impressionable into their cultish orbit. We would hear horror stories of classmates who'd ended up wed at sixteen, and with four kiddies hanging off their long skirts by the time they were twenty.

If you wanted a parent-sanctioned social life, the best option was the church youth club. You might have to put up with happy clappies, the occasional outbreak of people speaking in tongues and every sentence being punctuated with 'Praise the Lord', but at least you got out. The youth camp at Woodend was a major victory: I had momentarily liberated myself from the intense scrutiny of one set of parents and a grandparent.

I managed to get face time, as it were, with a Dutch boy with eyes as blue as the sea and have my first kiss, not to mention getting held up and robbed. I was walking along the beach feeling terribly pleased with myself in my newly patched jeans and groovy leather belt when a female friend and I were set upon by what we imagined were a pack of lesbian thugs staggering drunk and half naked out of the dunes. The biggest one seized my friend in a head grip and demanded I hand over my jeans and belt or else they'd give her the bash. After some fast talking we came out of it unbashed and with my jeans still intact, but the belt had had to be given up.

On September 28, 2011, Woodend Beach was, apart from a dog-walking couple who were unaware of the dire pseudo biblically endorsed warnings, completely devoid of people. It reminded me of the post-apocalyptic book cover of *On the Beach* by Nevil Shute and I hurried back to the car feeling too alone for comfort.

It wasn't until a week later that I realised why the date had seemed so significant. It wasn't the threat of quakes and tsunamis that had writ September 28 large in my brain. It was my mother's birthday. I had completely forgotten it, even though thoughts of her had been flooding my mind for days.

A few weeks ago CERA chief Roger Sutton announced that public bus tours of the Red Zone were in the planning stages and would be happening sometime in the near future. There is every expectation the queues will snake around Hagley Park and back again so you wonder how they'll manage the numbers. Will they work alphabetically through the phone book? Will we have to put our names into a hat? Will we have to pay more for a window seat? And will there be counsellors at the finish line to help us cope with the huge psychological shift we'll have to make after seeing the Forbidden City turned into a flattened wasteland?

A friend has returned to her workplace near the art gallery and is outraged that those coming to work in the inner city are still being charged pre-February 22 prices for car parks. She has a point. Apart from the art gallery gift shop, a cheesemonger and a couple of cafés, what is there on offer in the inner city anymore to warrant the council charging prices that would be fair enough only in a fully functioning city?

Exposing oneself

OCTOBER 17 – Just when I was asking myself, 'Where have all the boy racers gone?' I stopped the bike to buy a bottle of water at a bakery, and while I was sitting outside swigging it back a couple of gas garçons plonked themselves down at the next table and proceeded to wax lyrical about the new expanses of 'primo flat' now available for burnouts.

You think you get used to the sight and sites of tear-downs, the empty holes left where buildings have been wholesale demolished, but I was still shocked to see the flattened area where the buses used to come to rest on the corner of Fitzgerald and Moorhouse Avenues. With so much land cleared and converted into vast vacant lots, it's as though there are mini versions of the Canterbury Plains smack bang in the middle of town. Perhaps we should dig up the concrete foundations and sew grass to raise sheep, or hire exotic animal species from Orana Wildlife Park to tenant the areas

Exposing oneself

and bring in punters for Quake & Critter tours, at least until the insurers and property developers get their bottle back.

Imagine hanging out the washing in an inner-city residential and having a giraffe lean over the fence to chew your smalls. A couple of hefty rhinos parked up to patrol the primo flat would put a dent in a boy racer's machine to challenge the most gifted panel beater.

Speaking of vacant spaces, three decades ago when I worked for the city council as a groundsperson cum gravedigger, my chum and I, the only girls on staff, were overseen by an avuncular chap who would pick us up from our digs in his work truck fitted with giant hoses and take us out to water newly planted trees in various small parks. To our great amusement one of the parks was called Ray Blank Park, and the park was indeed very blank back then; we stood in our overalls directing the hoses in what seemed the middle of nowhere, giving the fledgling trees a drink. We wondered who Ray Blank was and marvelled at such an existential last name combined with such a kiwi first name.

Over the years I often spared a wistful thought for Ray Blank Park and wondered where it had got to. In fact, of course, it was always there, minding its own existential business, as I discovered while out riding shotgun on Saturday afternoon with a female friend who is big on home improvements and was picking up things secondhand to rectify post-quake wreckage. Caught short, my friend suddenly pulled over to the side of the road, relieved to have found the convenience of the Ray Blank Park ablution block. What was once the middle of nowhere had become very much the centre of somewhere on that side of the unbuckled town. The park looked quite the grown-up business, proudly sporting great towering leafy trees.

The day, which had started out cold, warmed up. As my friend hopped out of the car at the recycling yard to make her purchases, she shed the leggings and long jumper she was wearing. As we are on the subject of exotic species, I noticed as she trotted past the passenger door that all male eyes had come to rest upon the phenomenon that has come to be referred to as the camel toe area. I tried to signal a meaningful glance to her nether regions, but alas she paid no heed and by the time she got back into the car she had caused a small sensation.

Having just read Caitlin Moran's book *How to Be a Woman*, in which Moran decries the practice of women and girls spending their hard-earned pennies on Brazilians or total deforestation of the pubic area, I suspect that waxing of that area has brought the camel toe into sharper relief. Maybe, like the near-extinct whale tail – the thong and tattoo that could be seen on the rear end of a female wearing low-rider jeans – the toe could become a fashion statement. Those leading the way could buy small camel-hair poufs to wear down there as the new must-have accessory.

In fact such an accessory would be retro rather than new. The pubic wig, more commonly known as the merkin, was first worn in 1617 by prostitutes who shaved their genitalia. I suppose Eve was there for the genesis, having worn the first

Exposing oneself

fig leaf number back in the year blank to cover her nakedness after the snake had led her up the garden path.

Benecio and I have both received generous brown paper parcels bearing a Kilbirnie, Wellington post stamp from an anonymous sender. I laid Benecio's next to him on the bed and took a snap of him with 'Benecio Bowron' written in bold, black, felt-tip pen; he has demanded it be framed and hung on his wall of fame. It is very kind and thoughtful of the sender but really, honestly, no more. It is turning our heads. And rest assured that we have, as my great-aunt was wont to say, an excellency of sufficiency.

I was talking the other day to Joan, an elderly lady who has been through all the big earthquakes. She was a hundred miles out of Napier in Tuai for the Hawke's Bay quake of '31. Ushered outside the classroom by her teacher, she and the rest of the class watched as the contents of a water tank tipped over the teacher's head.

She was a wife and mother living in Inangahua on the West Coast for the one in '68, and forty years later in Christchurch, when September 4 came, she stayed in bed unperturbed. On February 22 she was residing on the second floor of the hospital and had to calm down a hysterical fellow patient as notes and paper flew about the air. She knows she's lucky to have come through the lot unscathed but has a deep acceptance of living alongside them. As Paul Newman said, 'Old age ain't for sissies.'

The new chic

OCTOBER 31 – The week has been full of big moments: a parade down Rolleston Avenue, with the public getting a close-up and personal view of the All Black heroes, and the opening up of sizeable chunks of the inner city.

The last time I remember lining Rolleston Avenue was on a rainy day when Liz the second cruised past in a long black car and we nippers got to see a flash of the royal gloved hand doing its thing. Decades later, Lorraine and I minced into town early enough to secure a good possie, plonking our backsides down on the grass and incurring decidedly damp hindquarters by the time the brass band heralded the pending approach of the ABs.

Everyone stood up and started to put on their game faces and organise their cheers, but by the time the first vehicle bearing the popes of the paddock arrived all the assembled seemed either too shocked to be in such close proximity to the gods, or too tongue-tied to come up with something appropriate to say. All, that is, except the schoolgirls who wove in front of the entourage flashing their orthodontic braces in the sun, giving their tonsils a thorough workout, and a private-school girl who waved a placard suggesting groin-injured Dan Carter could use hers any time.

I couldn't get over how regular-sized the ABs were. As I had once come around the corner of Princess Bay in Wellington to see Jonah Lomu in the process of removing his shirt and revealing a torso that could only be described as manly in a Schwarzenegger kind of a way, the victors of the Webb Ellis looked decidedly mortal. I blame the proliferation of oversized gym muscles in the wider public.

I heard myself yelling out, 'How's the leg doing, Aaron?' as Cruden sat in the back of a truck with his limb bound up in a state-of-the-art splint, and asking the same thing of DC, who appeared relaxed and in his element holding the golden cup. Meanwhile, Richie McCaw looked pale and exhausted, like a nouveau knight who had just returned from the Crusades and hadn't had time to catch his breath, let alone have his wounds attended to.

For the rest of the length of the avenue we could pretty much walk alongside the vehicle carrying the triumvirate of Dan, Richie and Ted: it moved at the pace of a medieval cart. The next day, after the ABs had paraded in Wellington, I turned on the TV news to see if Christchurch had turned out enough of the faithful to outdo the thousands in the capital. We hadn't.

The opening of Christchurch's central city retail precinct on Saturday was a miracle, kick-started from ground zero in the space formerly known as Cashel Mall. My spiritual home of Ballantynes is back up and running, and feeling slightly intoxicated after a reunion lunch I ventured into the swish new Persil-white makeup hall and recklessly applied green eye shadow, resulting in eyes the colour of the French first five's after Richie McCaw took him out in the World Cup final.

By the time I got there it was late in the day but the precinct was still jostling with shoppers straining at the bit to make a purchase, or just nosying among the new curiosity shops in their coloured containers. The people who created this have done a great job. I can't remember what was there before and to make an exact replica would have been disturbing, but it was lovely to see the trees from the previous era still standing to attention. With the low-rise maximum height of only two containers, there is now far more sunlight, the scale is more village-friendly and there is a proliferation of outside seating.

Johnson's greengrocer seemed entirely at home in the new setting. Kathmandu was in the mix after being Kathmandon't-ed over in Lichfield Street, and it was reassuring to have Scorpio Books there to give presents of mind, even if there was a glaring absence of more affordable shops – a Glassons or even a chemist – to entice punters across the board.

Sitting in a café, I overheard the owner effusively tell patrons that if they had come yesterday they would have seen a building site, and if they had come early that morning they would also have seen a building site, so down to the wire was the opening deadline. A terminally gormless man interrupted. 'Did you say this is a building site, mate?' I suppose if you had just come out of the bush, stumbled into the mall, and were none the wiser about its tragic backstory, you would be somewhat bewildered to be greeted with a confluence of container chic.

Meanwhile, down at the end of the new territorial lines of the Forbidden City, the Grand Chancellor leans on to live another grisly day. It and the other surviving skyscrapers seem so very last millennium.

High visibility

NOVEMBER 7 – Without wanting to sound like a paragraph out of a Jilly Cooper novel, I had decided to spend my morning riding and eating before having another nosey at the new Cashel Street container mall. Biking down Fitzgerald Avenue I noticed out of the corner of my eye a new eatery. I pulled over, dismounted, as Jilly would say, and went in to put on the nosebag.

It was a beautiful day so I decided to sit outside and was happily reading the paper when there was a sudden sound of crunching. As I watched, a four-wheel-drive with nobody in it drifted backwards, connected with the corner of the wall, ripped off a side mirror and scraped its flank before coming to rest a couple of feet away.

I looked through the window into the café and saw a group of high-visibility-jacketed men having a good old laugh. Gosh, I thought, they seem to be taking it rather well. Undeterred,

I returned to my task of ploughing through a bagel, before looking up to see a chap looking both amazed and sheepish at the same time. He walked around the car, scratching his head, and then said to me, 'Were you sitting just there?' nodding to the table next to the car.

'No,' I said, 'I was here.'

He looked at me incredulously, trying to insert me into his unfortunate narrative, and said, 'Did you not think to say anything?'

'Well, I looked through the window and saw you chaps laughing away and admired your cavalier attitude,' I said, determined not to feel as if I'd done anything wrong.

He shook his head at me, got back into the car and drove off, leaving me to examine my reaction, or lack of it.

I came to the following conclusions:

One, the car had gone as far as it could and wasn't going any further so it wasn't going to harm anyone or thing.

Two, as I am not the driver nor the owner of the car, nor the owner's wife, child or mother, I should not be admonished.

Three, in my experience, if a woman in a high state of animation rushes into a room full of blokes to announce that one of their machines has come to grief she is labelled a drama queen.

Four, after over 7,500 aftershocks, a car making a bid for freedom in a small semi-industrial car park doesn't rate in the grand scale of disasters.

Five, perhaps I was a little, shall we say, *disconnected* from the reality of it, cut off from the natural impulse to run inside and raise the alarm, and should not have so quickly assumed the driver was au fait with the situation outside. But for all I know he could have cardiac-arrested and slumped sideways on to his seat.

In my defence, growing up with brothers and no sisters, if I showed any inclination toward female hysteria I was highly ridiculed. Nevertheless, I would hate to think of myself as a bad citizen. Perhaps I should have caught the car in my arms, made a citizen's arrest, thrown myself over its bonnet.

Or maybe I've become a self-absorbed, insular git – correction, gittess. I see now that I had made the error of drifting into deeply male territory – as so much of Christchurch is now – where blokes belt up the roads in great mastodons of trucks on their way to perform their secret men's business.

On the way home I passed another café that used to be quite swanky. It was now colonised by all manner of four-wheel-drives and utes parked up on its forecourt, with men in hard hats and high vis jackets inside tucking into pies, and sandwiches as high as the Grand Chancellor. Pull up at a set of lights these days and there is usually a guy leaning one of his truck-driver arms out the window with a half-eaten pie on the end of it, suggesting pie-makers in this town must be making an absolute killing.

In my local café they're offering a free coffee for your high vis. Apparently there's even a High Vis Ball about to happen. I imagine it would be easy to dress for this, unlike togging up for the races, where is exercised possibly the worst-taste dress code in modern-day existence. Why do women spend truckloads each year on outfits that are anachronistic variations on mother-of-the-bride frocks? Or shell out for flimsy fascinators that end up after the last race looking like something Adam wore over his dried arrangements on a hot day in the Garden of Eden?

The announcement of bus trips through the Red Zone at the weekend had me on the phone on the dot of eight Wednesday morning. I finally managed to get through on the CERA 0800 number after ringing constantly for forty minutes. The receptionist said she'd try the lines to book the bus trip, did so three times, then came back and told me to try later.

I did so at various intervals throughout that day and the next, only to keep hearing the recorded voice message that I had phoned CERA after hours and could not leave a message. I was never fortunate enough to get an answer from the six lines installed to cope with the inundation of bookings: apparently each booking takes ten minutes to process because there's so much health and safety to be talked through.

With every expectation there would be vast numbers wanting a seat on the bus, why use the CERA number? Why not set up another phone line, or sell tickets in a special queue down at the bus station? With only weekends available for the bus trips, and their running for a limited period of time, it looks as though people will miss out, incurring further wrath and frustration from the public, who have run out of patience and want and need entrance to the Forbidden City.

Revelations

NOVEMBER 14 – I finally got a seat on the media bus the day the ChristChurch Cathedral was deconsecrated. It felt more than a little weird catching a bus into Cathedral Square. In the olden days I was always able to down tools and drift into town on shank's pony.

The bus left from Gloucester Street outside the art gallery and turned right at Cranmer Square to travel past what used to be my favourite inner-city piece of Christchurch, Victoria Square. Its grounds now looked ridden-hard and left-out-wet from liquefaction, neglect, and the wear and tear of deconstruction.

The coach driver was an A to B kind of a guy, so the rubbernecking down Colombo Street to those parts of Gloucester Street that have been concealed since February 22 yielded only the merest flash of a glimpse before we disembarked outside the cathedral. It was a freezing cold day and the microphones stood like twigs in the desolate landscape in front of the crumble of the cathedral. When the choir turned up you hoped they had thermals under their Crusader-red cassocks, but they were in fine voice and if the cold wind didn't raise a shiver down your spine the purity of their voices did. I spotted a lone man in a high visibility jacket and hard hat walking along the roof of the post office looking as sinister as a sniper and thanked God I wasn't a Kennedy.

Timing is everything. At the very moment the dean uttered his final words, drawing the service to a conclusion and turning the cathedral and its grounds from sacred to secular, a construction worker near the BNZ building was heard to yell out, 'Take your hands off me!' as a clutch of hard hats quickly moved to break up a fight. It was as if the land, which had tolerated the religion of the cathedral since the early 1880s, had suddenly taken possession of the construction worker's tongue to herald the building's liberation from its holy inhabitants.

Looking around the square I was surprised to see how many buildings stood, but shocked to hear how many were still to come down. It is hard to imagine where you would begin the strategic attack on these enormous edifices. The ugly BNZ House is to tumble, as is the Government Life building. I clearly remember as a child the excitement of standing outside Government Life watching the new digital clock change time. My mother toiled in one of the tall buildings in the square in her first job after she left school at fourteen, working as a dental mechanic for a boss with the fabulous name of Cornelius Polglase Brandon Tripe. She would often regale us with the story of a farmer bringing in his young wife and instructing the dentist to extract all her teeth and replace them with a set of dentures. My mother was horrified to look down on the square and see, post op, the farmer's wife lying prone in the back of a truck against a pile of sacks, nursing a hurt bruised mouth for the unceremonious drive home.

Alas, the Chancery Arcade is no more, but it had gone to seed years ago and was a far cry from its heyday, when it housed the bohemian Number 17 Coffee Lounge with its waxy candles in bottles in an attempt to recreate a Dickensian atmosphere.

Then there is the cathedral itself, and its founding urban myth of the miscreant who climbed the spire, dropped a penny over the side, and watched with glee as it penetrated the skull of an innocent passerby.

It was always worth poking your nose into the cathedral at Christmas to see – as we did (and will still do) with Ballantyne's shop windows – what theme they'd run with for the nativity scene. Once I had to play Joseph in my school's nativity play in the cathedral. The Aged Parents thought it a huge joke that their daughter at an all-girls' school had been burly enough to land the male lead. Decades later I'm old and ugly enough, but not sage enough, to play one of the Three Wise Men.

Piggy and other bad dreams

NOVEMBER 21 – The best thing about recurring dreams is waking up from a cold sweat to find it was only your subconscious busy on the job processing issues about which your conscious mind is none the wiser. I'm embarrassed to have used the hideous expression 'processing issues' but there you go. How else do you explain the wasted meandering narrative of dreams?

For years I have been afflicted with a dream where I'm still in the sixth form wearing a kilt and hoping no one will notice how many rings there are round my trunk. Another culprit who puts in a regular appearance – and I know I share this with many – is walking round in public with no underpants on, desperately trying to find them but being sidetracked by various pressing engagements. Yet another, which popped up a couple of days ago, is about being in a play: the curtains are about to go up and I do not have a clue what the lines are.

Now the latest recurring dream – I suppose I can classify it as that because I've had it twice – is that I am frantically trying to get to a voting booth but being endlessly delayed along the way. Having spent the last few months haranguing anyone unfortunate enough to listen about how important it is to exercise your franchise, and having secured a seat on a Red Zone bus on the same day as the election, I'm irrationally worried that I won't make it back from the bus trip in time to get to the polling booth.

I am shocked when people breezily tell me they're not voting, have never voted, and have no intention of voting in the foreseeable future, the usual excuse being that 'they' are all a pack o' bastards and there's no one who represents the person's position. 'Well sorry, it's not a perfect world', I say, and tub-thump about the history of the franchise: how in England a suffragette threw herself under the king's horse in protest over not having the vote and was killed; how blacks in South Africa got the vote only in the '90s … trala trala trala.

Having been brought up in a household where excitement built during the campaign weeks and peaked with the glory of election night, when we filled in the special newspaper printout as each result came in, next Saturday, a date that comes around only once every three years, is my equivalent of the World Cup. I don't care what people vote for as long as they get off their backsides and perform their democratic right, because it is precious and was hard fought for.

My parents were dyed-in-the-wool National Party voters; they met as Junior Nats, debating on opposite sides. However, when we came along Dad had the decency to cart us around the traps during election campaigns to attend a cross section of political party meetings. As was the case with most of their generation, they brought up three liberal thinkers. We all voted differently, the one united thing in the family being a deep loathing of and ridicule for the Social Credit Party and Bruce Beetham's crimplene suits.

I remember the day Jack Marshall came to our house and lay down on the marital bed for an afternoon nap before attending a meeting, and my mother wanting to erect a plaque: 'Gentleman Jack lay here'. And I vividly remember, as a teenager, meeting that strange adventure Piggy Muldoon in the flesh and being amazed at the absolutely enormous size of his head, suspecting alien parenting must have been involved.

What is there not to like about election night, about watching history unfold and knowing you had a tiny part in the making of it? What's not to like about all the drama, the cameras trained on the two main party leaders' houses, reporters looking for the merest twitch in the curtains, the cathode glare of a television being avidly watched as the results pour in, the great excitement when the next prime minister finally opens the front door and gets into a car that speeds off to HQ, the leader arriving, parting the sea of the party faithful to mount the podium and make the acceptance speech, being joined by awkward family members thrust into the spotlight?

What's not to like about keenly watching the other glum camp to see how soon the loser calls the victor to acknowledge defeat and offer congratulations – which, in turn, the winner must make special mention of.

I know I don't get out much, but in spite of the polling of the electorate every five minutes by the media, the obscenity of the marketing and branding, and the ghastly personality politics, I find election night deeply moving. Not a week passes without it crossing my mind how lucky I am to be a woman born in this country where we were the first to get the vote, what a privilege it is. So next Saturday, however hungover you may feel, however busy your calendar is, however disenchanted you are with the system, go on ya mug, have a go and vote please.

The last goodbye

NOVEMBER 28 – I had just heard on the radio that the first two hours of voting on election day were supposed to be the heaviest, so I sauntered down to Christchurch East School to join the queue and was astonished to discover that in the cavernous hall there were only five of us doing the business.

When the scrutineer located me on the electoral roll and ran the ruler and red pen through my name, I saw with alarm that, on the two pages in front of her, my name was the only one crossed out. It was already midday. On my way out I slapped a sticky badge on my sleeve to say I'd voted in the faint hope of encouraging others. I did not see anyone else wearing one the entire day.

Everyone I talked to had had a similar experience, so when I heard the next morning that voter turnout was the lowest since the 1880s, with only sixty-five percent bothering to exercise their franchise, I wasn't at all surprised. Sure, the quakes may have taken out a few old familiar polling booths, but the city was well signposted with arrows all over the place to entice in the punters. With my electorate of Christchurch Central currently in a dead heat between Nicky Wagner and Brendon Burns, I hope those who were too lazy or blasé to vote are kicking themselves now they know their vote could have been critical.

So, why the low turnout? Maybe it's true that the brightest and the best have quit New Zealand, leaving behind the dumb and disenfranchised and those who can still afford the lifestyle choice of living in the unlucky country. Everyone predicted a further swing to National but not even Labour's biggest detractors would not have imagined the gothic horror that unfolded on Saturday night as the party shed a quarter of a million votes.

After I had been to the ballot box I went around to the Garage People's new headquarters and walked with Lorraine to Cranmer Square to take the bus into the Red Zone, which she had kindly booked for us three weeks earlier. Amazingly, there were still some incredibly stupid people milling about the square in flimsy footwear and thinking all they had to do was rock up on a whim to score a seat.

When speaking to journalists who'd been on this Red Zone tour, some of them several times, I had been constantly amazed me by their lack of description of what they'd seen. It is a cliché to say that words failed me, but as my mind struggled to absorb the carnage I understood why they had been so mute.

I also realised that, although I am one of the 'donut' people living on the outskirts of the Red Zone, I have been in lala land, imagining a rebuild and brave new world. It was truly disturbing to see the scale of the demolition, of what we have lost, of what has been eradicated from the face of the Earth. The grand-scale levelling of the CBD has turned it into a giant gap-filler landscape.

The bus stopped outside the Pyne Gould Guinness and CTV building sites for a few respectful minutes, but the guy holding the microphone should have been telling us what streets we were entering and what buildings used to be there, as we kept quickly turning our heads left and right and asking each other, 'What was there?' and 'Where are we now?'

Several times before we entered the Red Zone we were asked if we wanted to get off the bus. Maybe I should have taken the opportunity. Halfway through the tour I was gripped with claustrophobia. I wanted to get away from the coated men with their clipboards, out into the fresh, undamaged air. I felt profoundly depressed, beyond sad, as my mind tried to rearrange the mental furniture and say goodbye to what had been and would never be again. I desperately wanted to get near New Regent Street which, rumour has it, has stood up well but the route didn't take us there.

As we poured off the bus at the end I felt physically and mentally shaken up, like a small child who'd tried to be brave and go on the scariest ride in the fairground. The organisers were handing out small cards with a number on them to ring if we wanted to talk about it. Nobody took one.

Summer on the grass

DECEMBER 5 – Christmas down here is noticeably low-key this year so it was disappointing to go into Ballantynes – the spiritual home – and see a large section devoted to yuletide baubles and paraphernalia. Don't get me wrong, I love the smell of Christmas pine needles and lilies, but do we really have to continue to buy into the repulsive consumerism of over-the-top decorations after having our world irrevocably shaken up? If we collectively sat on Father Christmas's knee and were asked what we really wanted for Christmas, I don't think it would be anything store-bought.

The last thing we need is retail-engineered stress and a big blowout that most can't afford. Ask people what they're doing this year for the holiday break and you get a uniform reply: everyone just wants to get the hell out of Shaky Town to relax and quietly process and sort through the baggage of 2011.

Speaking of blowouts and expense, Benecio has been

under the knife again to remove a growth from the eye and has also had five fangs extracted, but I must say he has made a sterling recovery. Used to keeping feline hours, I am now woken several times in the early morning by licks to the eyelids from Himself wanting the fridge door opened and a bleary wrestle with the tin opener to sate his hunger pangs. He's on notice that if this incessant demand feeding keeps up I'll have to elasticise the waistband of his trousers.

Watching the dismantling of the Grand Chancellor Hotel is like observing an old-fashioned stripper slowly disrobing from top to bottom. Floor by floor, you see the concrete go and the living daylights shine through. You can get a really good look at it from fashion-designer-chic NG. This building was closed as it is in the Red Zone, but craftily the owners had the grand old building reinforced and recently resituated its entrance at the back. Talk about literally thinking outside the square. On opening night it was quite a spectacle seeing elegantly dressed women stalk through the rubble, walk up the ramp and enter the high-studded interior to peruse shoes and racks of what I would call intellectual, mostly black, designer threads with eye-watering price tags.

Things seem to be happening at quite a pace. A neighbour arrived at the back door with a clutch of poppies and sweet peas from a deserted section to tell me that the street one road over can now be driven through all the way. And that in a matter of days a huge one-storey central city library is opening just a stone's throw away in Peterborough Street, opposite the Strawberry Fare restaurant.

What a mecca Strawberry Fare was to the Aged Parents, who dined there every Sunday lunch and had the same dish and the same glass of wine waiting for them, thanks to the obliging staff. The journey there was made with military precision; my father would look at his watch before commanding us to get into the car to make sure we'd arrive at exactly ten minutes to noon 'to beat the rush'.

As my mother, with her many infirmities, was extricated from her car seat my father, hands clasped behind his back, would stare up the road, keeping a lookout for my brother the vicar to appear, and on spotting him would announce, 'I see His Grace has arrived.'

Inside, my mother, advanced in her dementia and imagining she was still a young thing, would laugh at the long tables patronised by grey- and white-haired women and say, 'Look at all the old ducks', while occasionally Dad would delight in throwing the maitre d' by ordering duck à l'orange to, as he pronounced, do his bit at keeping down the population on the Avon.

That building is made of red brick and, like many grumpy old buildings that threw a wobbly in the quakes, is in a state of repair. How I wish it were again a going concern, but as a friend sagely remarked after we were ruminating on the battering taken by the inner city, when a vase is broken you can never really put it back together again the same way.

Over in Chester Street East the two sections that were bought by the council before the quake with plans to make them into a park have been sown with grass seed and there is now great excitement to actually see the green baize coming up. So summer is here, the grass is riz, and I look forward to that happy day when we can take a picnic and rug to the park and do a Joni, as in Mitchell, to enjoy the hissing of summer lawns.

Sporting red

DECEMBER 12 – It seems only a short time ago that everyone was up in arms when the Christchurch City Council appeared to be frittering away valuable resources employing groundspeople to garden and mow in the abandoned Red Zone. Now that we have been given increased access to what has gone down, and is going on, in the zone and can see grass that's grown sometimes as high as the park benches, we are lamenting the let-go, overgrown appearance of the interior. Perhaps when the grass is cut it could be marketed as Red Zone Hay and sold online to raise money for the rebuild.

Getting one's head around the visual assault in Christchurch is an ongoing process. Expecting long queues and a substantial wait for a walking tour from the end of Cashel Street Mall into Cathedral Square, I was surprised on Saturday morning to be waved straight through for a gold coin donation. The natural impulse when standing behind the metal cordons to peer at the devastation down High Street is to loop your fingers through the wire mesh, which makes you feel like a prisoner, or a zoo visitor on the other side of the fence.

Marrying what is with what was when these now deserted streets teamed with busy pedestrians and traffic takes a leap in understanding. As we near the end of the calendar year and grow quietly confident in the absence of significant aftershocks, there is an expectation that the violent calamities of the year will gain perspective, be parked somewhere, put in a box. Who won't hesitate before raising a New Year glass at the bitter end and expressing a wish for a better year than the last? After all, isn't that what we said last year?

There's a lot of processing going on in our collective subconscious. It's heartening to notice how appreciative you become of any signs of new life and beginnings, whether it's the opening of a café, pub or library or finding a favourite old shop relocated miles away. It is strange to visit Old Stumpy Square, as the wizard calls it, and see brand new perspectives revealed with the removal of buildings. I had never before noticed the surreal painted exterior of the Millennium Hotel, which makes you feel dizzy if you look at it too long, or the brutality and ugliness of most of the modern buggered buildings that are due to come down.

I gave a bum steer to a friend who migrated to Christchurch just in time for the nasty June belt but had not yet experienced a summer here. During last week's hot balmy weather she asked me if it was like this all the time. 'Oh yes,' I told her airily. 'It will remain like this right through until March.'

Yeah right. This week has been chilly and rainy. I dropped off an old mate visiting from Wellington in a street that had taken some hits. As he slammed the car door, a Mr Whippy ice-cream van lurched down the lane, wildly singing 'Greensleeves' in a sinister fashion as trees swung around madly. The wind spirited away from the washing line a fitted sheet that had seen better days, providing an excuse for retail therapy. I found a set of cardinal red sheets and two pillowcases of high quality knocked down to $39. Having never before owned red sheets, I had to be egged on to the purchase by my offsider, who informed me red sheets are very empowering to sleep in. And indeed, when I fitted them to the bed and jumped in feeling quite the Borgia, I had a wild impulse to phone Jeremy Irons and tell him to come on over and don't forget the execution papers.

I've noticed inner-cityites sporting badges that say 'A Vibrant Stayer' in Crusader red and black. Not being a badge sort of person, I feel I'm doing my bit with the red sheets, and black and white Benecio looks dramatic sprawled out across them.

Simon from the relocated Garage People has transformed a grotty back garden, chocker with rubbish, into a veritable oasis of order, planting rows of vegetables with lines of bricks laid down between each row. It makes our garden look like a dog's breakfast but we will see in a few weeks' time which camp will bear the greater crop. I ask him if I can bring a mate over to admire his handiwork and he gives me a slow grin.

'By all means,' he says, 'for a small gold coin donation.'

Nativity scenes

DECEMBER 19 – If you are an early riser and go for a bike ride round the inner city when no one's around, it's easy to be overwhelmed by the eeriness and imagine you're alone in the aftermath. A few days ago, just after sunrise, I was biking down Colombo Street heading for the new Cashel Street mall when my ears were assaulted by the obnoxiously loud sound recording that accompanies the nativity scene in Ballantynes' front windows. I know that in various parts of the world cities have used Barry Manilow and other similarly aurally vulgar music to disperse errant mobs from malls. After listening to this, I reckon it could do the trick.

One glance at Mary, Joseph and a crazy-eyed donkey, all doing their level best to look the nativity part, and you can understand from their ravaged features why they're suffering from last-stage sleep deprivation. Ditto the Three Wise Men, who seem to be unhinged manic comic turns thoroughly up to no good. Whoever fashioned these strange figurines must be having a good laugh somewhere because they've come up with characters who could be close cousins of The Missing Link. A not-too-close inspection of Mary's face and you can see why she was still a virgin.

In reference to things loud, I nearly fell off my seat the other morning at a café when the courteous manager asked me if I would object to music playing quietly in the background or prefer silence.

'Silence,' I replied stunned by her consultation, and then launched into a diatribe about traumatic visits to cafés where seemingly oblivious staff are in the habit of turning up their wretched personal choice of music full bore. Never mind the customer, you think, as you wait for your coffee and try to read the newspaper as some rapper bangs on about his Mother F****** day. Struggling to shriek over the music and the clatter of the coffee machinery to talk to a cobber leaves you feeling wrung out and exhausted, a day older than the God particle.

Controversy continues to rage over the rebuild of the cathedral and the proposed expensive temporary replacement made of cardboard. Then along comes a wunderkind, eleven-year-old Ben Jensen of Waikari, who knocks up a pint-sized replica of the cathedral out of corrugated iron. Why not follow suit and rebuild the cathedral in that affordable hard-case DIY kiwi material and save the city millions? In fact, why not rebuild all the butt-ugly doomed buildings in the square in corrugated iron so people can flock from far and wide to observe the commonsense solution and debate the aesthetic merits of the container mall and corrugated iron square? While we're at it, let's do without the craven cathedral shop, filled with questionable taste cathedral paraphernalia, through which visitors were compelled to walk as it was the only exit. Questions were raised about this perilous one-way route after the February quake.

The Deaf Association building, the last to come down at our Kilmore Street intersection, has been done quick smart; we watched the pincers of the bulldozer smash into perfectly recyclable double doors and windows. So much waste, carted off to a dump. One wonders what will come in its place: apparently the rebuild of our intersection is going to happen within two swift years. It will be a great boost to get the dairy back. The last one specialised in bananas, enormous tins of fish, and lashings of Kronic, but at least it was only a merciful dash across the road to get a loaf of bread, albeit white and limp.

I visit a solo mum living over in Shirley in a Housing New Zealand flat. For ten months since the February quake she has had to put up with a pile of pooh, mixed with liquefaction, that turned up in her backyard and made the lawn a no-go area for her small child, who has had to remain inside. The 27-tonne hill delivered an unrelenting pong, especially on a windy day. Finally this week a bulldozer turned up and took it away. She will at last be able to remove the peg from her nose.

This summer has brought a profusion of Flanders Fields' poppies, great red splashes of the delicate flower fiercely springing up everywhere and reminding you of those who died in the quake. Down at Pomeroy's pub there is no sign of one of the regulars, an American Christian MP who came to Christchurch to help run the earthquake recovery. Even though this man opposed gay marriage he advertised his seminal services to lesbian couples, unbeknown to his wife back home. Apparently his donations exceeded the clinic limit so perhaps he's taking a break from the hops to raise the sperm count. It's a brave new world.

More skew-whiffery

DECEMBER 26 – All Thursday night Benecio pestered me, wanting me to get out of bed and feed him, and he was in my face most of Friday morning. I fed him once, twice, three times. I found his brush, which usually seems to calm him down, with the combing drawing huge clumps of fur. Miriam, who is nearly as obsessed with the boy as I am, came over and I said, 'Thank god you're here to sort out the lad. He's being very intense. I do hope that doesn't mean there's another quake coming.' 'Don't say that,' she said.

By the time she left he was sitting curled up on the couch sleeping like a baby and I was banging away on the keyboard, trying to get all the work done before Friday ended. Then Old Bucky did his block and threw a wobbly. It felt as violent as the February earthquake. Benecio shot outside and I staggered after him. Then there was a smaller one. I went to the garage, wrenched the door open, got out the bike and was just about to leave when I saw Lorraine walk up the drive. Her face was the colour of white enamel. I dropped the bike and went to her.

We dragged chairs from wherever we could as more people arrived and sat down around the front lawn. There was plenty of liquor in the house in preparation for Christmas so we broke it open and had the mandatory stiff one before the next big one hit.

Usually when you sit outside during the aftershocks you don't feel them as much. Not this time, this time it felt biblical, as if the Earth were going to open up and we were going to fall into it. A lot of whites were being shown in eyes as we rocked and rolled with the beast, before it unclenched its grasp and drew breath again.

The power went out and came back on. I filled up watering cans and milk bottles, even though I had plenty of water in reserve and a stream has opened up under the house and been rerouted into a drain we can access in time of need.

The staff from Beat Street Café drifted past the fence, leaned over and said there'd been a bit of damage, and we invited them in. More chairs were found and I went inside and got the laptop; I then walked around with it in stunned mullet fashion, poking at the 'on' switch aimlessly, not able to able to get it going.

The landlord and landlady arrived and with more numbers came more strength. Some of us grew silent, some of us had flashbacks to February, some talked manically, some of us wept.

More skew-whiffery

I went to bed with Benecio next to me. Later, I got up in the dark, sat in Dad's old chair and stared at the skew-whiffery of the walls and the mess on the floors, and Benecio came through and hid under the desk. There was a knock at the door and I was pleased to see Eve there; we sat and debriefed, going through the terrors of the afternoon.

After she left I got back into bed *avec* cat, but when the 5.1 hit at seven-thirty a.m. he bolted and hasn't been since, and neither have the other cats in the compound. Whatever secret cat bolt-hole they go to, I just wish they'd come back.

I stayed in bed late and thought: what's the point of getting up? Normally after a shock I want to get in the shower in case it's my last for a while but not today. To state the bleeding obvious, this has completely done in what little we had left of our munted heads, but at least all that has fallen down has fallen down, minimalising the Chicken Licken threat.

I hunt for my Australian-based brother's phone number in my book and go into a frenzied panic when I can't find it. Scrambled eggs for brains: I see it staring at me right in front of my fat face. Come back, Benecio, normal transmission has been restored. We live to fight another Old Bucky day.

Indomitability

JANUARY 2 – Three times I have taken cabs leaving from Kilmore Street and had to tell the drivers that, yes, you *can* travel down the road all the way to Manchester Street. Even though this has been the case for weeks, it appears to be news to them as they back out of the drive and start to swing east in the direction of Fitzgerald Avenue so they can eventually travel west.

You'd think there would be a system in place for cab companies to share updated information with drivers about the reopening of roads, or perhaps I seem quite the colossal chump who will put up, shut up and cough up for the longer drive. Ask cab drivers how business has been since February and they say it's never returned to what it was because people don't want to, or can't, pay for longer journeys due to road closures. Surely it's not too much to expect it to be every taxi driver's right and proper duty to know the city and its circuits like the back of his or her hand, rather than rely on surly residents, suspicious of being ripped off, to tell them which way is up?

News that the water pipes are further compromised after the December 23 quakes will soon put paid to the watering of gardens. What a pity, just when the tomatoes and courgettes are flowering and the lettuces are strong of leaf. It would be a damn shame and a waste of communal effort to watch the plants slowly perish. There's always the stream that sprang up under the house: we may be able to trot cuploads of water from it across to the patch so we mustn't give up hope yet. It brings such simple pleasure to see things grow in this – as crooner Gene Pitney once sang – town without pity.

Benecio is back but unfortunately has turned into the proverbial scaredy cat and will only come into the house at night to feed. At the merest rattle he loses his bottle and tears off outside. I had really thought he might return indoors with the rain. I so miss looking across the room at him curled up with a smile on his dial at the endless admiration of which he was on the receiving end. I note that his paws, which once proudly resembled an immaculate pair of black and white spats, are getting grubby as he turns slowly feral. He doesn't want to come home because he thinks the flat is a place where bad things happen so I must be grateful for any visit, no matter how brief. If only I could explain things, talk to the animals.

All the books in the newly opened central city library in Peterborough Street broke their quake restraints and fell off the shelves, so the place remained closed for an extra public holiday as dejected library-goers read the notice and trudged away with their unreturned books. The day the library opened I felt like shedding a municipally proud tear seeing staff briskly administer to customers' requests and flash welcoming smiles.

The entire back row devoted to laptop computers was populated by youthful card-carrying library members quietly pounding the keyboards, eyes glazed to the screen. Two boys of Fatty and Skinny dimensions sat cheek by jowl on a couch, totally lost in the books balanced on their laps. I felt like taking a photograph to record the rare sighting but it would have been churlish to interrupt their deep absorption.

My friend from Australia, accompanying me on my walk to the library after having satisfied her curiosity about Latimer Square, kept remarking how quiet the streets were, that we had passed only a handful of people. Now it really is quiet after Bride of Bucky took another piece out of us on that horrible Friday; everyone has decamped the shocking city.

When Civil Defence in Wellington heard stories post February of how the inner-city residents of Christchurch had their doors kicked in by staff absurdly following to the letter orders to enter houses to check for the dead or those in need of help, they came up with a cunning plan. They have trained a handful of staff to gently pick locks, rather than roughly break and enter properties, and have also made available for the sum of five dollars three-litre water containers as the bigger ones are too heavy to lift. Apparently, if you fill the

Indomitability

container to brimming-over level and then put the cap on and keep said container in a dark place, the water will keep for a year without your having to resort to belts of bleach. And don't use milk containers: they contaminate the water.

Remember ninety-three-year-old Joseph about whom I wrote some months ago after meeting him in the freeze of winter when, without power, he was battling on in his rented boarding-house room with only an outside toilet? He spent this Christmas in hospital with pneumonia. His mate across the landing had checked on him one night, found him marooned on the floor and lifted him back into bed. When I visited him in hospital he looked considerably frailer than last time and, as a chest-gurgling cough gripped his slight frame, talked of four days being left on the floor.

He's a lesson to all of us in his indomitable fight for life. If he goes into care, hopefully it will be somewhere close by in the inner city so he can still walk around the traps in his old familiar hood. He talks of wanting to get home and plant his apple cucumbers and insists he's still up for it, not down or out, still in the game.

'I'm like Oliver Twist,' he told me as I frowned, not understanding. He laughed painfully, rattling the muck in his chest, before explaining, 'I'm the old boy who asked for more.'

Entrepreneurs

JANUARY 9 – With these five-pointer-plus shakes that keep pounding the city, even the more solid buildings that were previously unscathed are beginning to show signs of wear and terror. If we were hyper-aware before, we are super-hyper-aware now and when the roads are clear of traffic I choose to walk out on the carriageway to avoid falling debris from dilapidated awnings. It's either that or permanently slapping on a bicycle or motorbike helmet while we wait for both our nerves and the ground to settle down.

Residential property owners, weary of trying to restore order to their premises, aren't bothering now. As you walk past you notice letterboxes, gates and fences on a permanent, insolent lean – off-centre poses of dilapidation. Who has energy left to constantly make a silk purse out of a sow's ear?

It's hard to believe around the inner city and affected suburbs that Christchurch was once called the Garden City, and control-freak gardeners slavishly dug, weeded, watered and landscaped, trying to impose order on Mother Nature. Now she's winning as ever more streets and houses are vacated, leaving behind wild growth and middle-aged to elderly men, too broken and broke to quit the city, walking aimlessly in zombie *Dawn Of The Dead* circuits. All that's missing is the tumbleweed. One wonders if those who left town to holiday in the sunless north or Wanaka and have heard about the quakes are seriously contemplating upping sticks and leaving the field, job or no job.

Since December 23 there has been a constant wail of sirens as fire trucks rush off to halt another arsonist at play putting a match to deserted properties. On top of the increasingly insurgent and odd behaviour, I recently observed a shifty bloke walking along Avonside Drive rifling through the mail in letterboxes and tossing what didn't interest him back over fences. The flow of any trip in a car is interrupted by police cars bursting into high-pitched song as they siren past, lights flashing, on the way to, one supposes, a burglary or a domestic incident. I pity them their exhaustion.

On Saturday morning I notice a flurry of activity going on at our intersection, on the land where the Piko building once stood. A high vis clipboard kind of a guy in charge of the gang tells me the people wordlessly swinging sledgehammers and breaking up bricks are American students over on a working holiday. It's all part of the Greening the Rubble project he says, and tells me that what's left of the Piko building will be strengthened and rented to a yoga outfit. There's so much rubble to green you wonder if there will be enough people left to enjoy the public spaces. Will those remaining get to wander the grounds like mental health patients in an al fresco asylum?

Perhaps we could turn the CBD into a giant Te Papa exhibit, no need for a pussy quake-simulator here, or advertise dandruff-free holidays. Even as we speak, entrepreneurs in the beauty industry may be experimenting with turning liquefaction into facial mud packs.

Everyone is obsessed with sleep. We ask each other (excuse the sordid overtones), 'How much did you get last night?' Benecio and I both have bags under our bleary eyes. The good news is that we have greatness living in our midst: Millie next door won the worldwide Lego Mock Olympics. After completing seven builds over three months, taking ten days per build, she took out the grand final with her construction of Aesop's fable *The Tortoise and the Hare*. At this rate she'll be doing Gerry Brownlee, the Fat Controller at CERA, out of a job; we tell her she should be overseeing the rebuild of the CBD.

In the belly of the whale

JANUARY 16 –When the five-point aftershock struck round three on Sunday morning I was amazed to observe Benecio manfully, or Maine Coonly, remain at his post on my bed as we waited for the rattling to cease and desist. Aha, maybe giving him drops of rescue remedy in his tucker, a tip a kind reader suggested to me, has had the desired effect.

I slapped on the radio for some soothing background music and wondered once again what the hell Old Bucky is up to as he keeps drifting north-east out to sea to who knows where – to hook up with the Kaikoura fault line perhaps? Then we'll all be done for.

It has been a week of drama. We were walking along Kilmore Street and had just passed Dawson Street when we glanced down and saw a man crawling along the lane, unable to get up. We tried to give him a hand up but whatever he was on, or whatever had happened to him, he was too hobbled to stand, too incoherent to communicate much to us except his name.

It was broad daylight and, displaying a cut on his forehead and bleeding hands, he looked the epitome of down and out, as if he'd just crawled from a hole in the ground. We dialled 111 for an ambulance. It took its time, but perhaps that's the way it seems when you're frantic and looking for help. The woman on the end of the line kept asking me what my number was over and over again, which seemed strange. Surely she would have had it right in front of her?

A car came down the lane and the driver got out and helped us prop the man up against the wall of the deserted building nicknamed The Lost Tribe of Albinos. The man became agitated, angrily spitting out that he'd left a pot of water boiling on the stove back at his place around the corner and was afraid the flat was going to catch fire. By the time the ambulance arrived I had imagined a house ablaze a few blocks away and babbled the information to the ambulance crew, who seemed relaxed to hear it. Then the police turned up, two young blokes in uniform and another intense chap all dressed in black. They didn't seem to know the man or be particularly concerned about his physical state, although one of the cops asked him if he'd broken his jaw. I guess it was just business as usual, another deadbeat turning up in a deadbeat town.

I felt sorry for the man, with several pairs of strangers' eyes all trained upon him, so I left and went home. The whole incident, happening upon this slight, strange figure in such a state of profound degradation and our ineffectual ministrations toward him, must have taken only about half an hour but it left me feeling shattered. I wondered what his life was like before and after the quakes, if he had any friends, where he was going, how old he was, and why his lips were so blue. The next morning I biked past the address he'd given to police and noted it was a slum dwelling, something you'd imagine seeing in Soweto, but there were clothes on the line so some sort of effort had been made. It registered, not for the first time in the past eighteen months, that there but for the grace of God go I.

Earlier in the week I ventured into the Red Zone with another journalist, a photographer and a helpful minder, all of us piled into the photographer's car. For most of the two-hour trip it felt as if we were the last souls left on Earth. Huge new fissures in the terra unfirma had opened up since December 23 on the cordoned-off stretch of Kilmore Street, including a drop in the car park on the lean of the Markham building. Flags flew defiantly on the Marque Hotel and the building that once housed Bob Brown's HiFi, and it was truly wonderful to see New Regent Street looking comparatively unscathed, but the rest of the CBD was so bleak and ravaged it felt as vast and empty as the belly of a whale.

The tear-down has and is being constantly filmed, photographed and written about but none of this captures the aesthetic triage that is going on. Painters and poets are sent into the big white of Antarctica to give their interpretation of that lonely inhuman landscape, so surely the unique interior of the Forbidden City might be captured and explained to us by artists and writers? The CBD, now turning into a landscape, would produce truly great art.

In Manchester Street we stopped the car, got out and looked up at the workers toiling away on the Grand Chancellor building. What terror it must be for them during the sizeable aftershocks to which we have been subjected, as they, neither up nor down, have to brace and bear it. About three brave souls were stalking the ramparts. I waved out to one and was moved to see him give a friendly wave back.

The trip came to an end in the square, outside the ongoing tragedy that is the cathedral. A food wagon for the workers emitted tantalising wafts of the big hit on their menu – hot rolls with roast beef or pork and gravy for a mere $6.50. Suddenly famished, we got one each and devoured them like starving animals. The couple operating the van told us they had decided, after the nastiness of December 23, that they had had enough. Living with Old Bucky is like living in a violent relationship: you never know if and when he's going to lash out next. He gives fractures, leaves black eyes of the soul, and everyone has their limit. So the couple is off to 'somewhere in Australia' to follow in the footsteps of their children.

Meanwhile, it is heartening to hear that the children who remain in Christchurch are taking the quakes in their small strides: they act out seismic dramas, build huts, shake them, start a rebuild, and strut around with clipboards doing EQC house inspections and shouting out, 'This house is condemned!'

Happy hour

JANUARY 23 – Last year I was in the water as early as October but this year it is only in the last two weeks that I have ventured into the brine, and boy do I feel all the better for it.

Apparently in the olden days mental hospitals would immerse patients with chronic depression into saltwater tanks because the salt was thought to cheer them up, although one can't help but think the confinement of the tanks would have done in the heads of the claustrophobics.

When I lived on Mt Pleasant it was just a mad sweaty dash through Lyttelton Tunnel to get to Corsair and Cass Bay or Rapaki, my salty watering holes of choice, but now it's quite a trek. There's always North Brighton, but in that neck of the woods even the slightest wind gust has you donning Lawrence of Arabia headgear to withstand the assault of sand blasts from the dunes.

I like my beaches sheltered and you'd be hard-pressed to find a beach more snuggled in from the elements than Corsair Bay. If you wonder where the boy racers have gone to since the bumps in the roads dealt to their chassis, ruining their hoonish play, you will find them parked up at Corsair, and the only trouble with this beach is that where you lay your towel is very cheek-by-jowl, so last time I was there I had to listen to about thirty minutes of uninterrupted discourse by a boy racer giving a glowing and boastful account of his latest shagging wagon.

Unable to stand another greasy minute of it, I decamped and walked up the steep path to the car park, where two beaten-up jalopies were bonnet to bonnet as the drivers ripped the air with their revs and obscenities until a genius came to the conclusion that one of the cars had a flat battery. Poor Corsair, I thought, what have you done to deserve this, such a beautiful spot to be so profoundly sullied by the uncouth? If this were an art installation of bogan-at-the-beach it would be called 'Oxymoronic', with the emphasis on moronic.

While we are on the topic of engine- and machine-worshippers, as a keen practitioner of anthropomorphism – for example 'Old Bucky' – it is heartening to note that the diggers and cranes have been given names. First the third largest digger in the world, boasting a 65-metre claw and going by the name 'Twinkle Toes', arrived to help with the demolition, and now we have the lofty 'Goliath', brought out to attack the hideous monstrosity that is the BNZ building.

Happy hour

Some find the naming of things non-human mawkish and sentimental, but I think it helps us cope, in this case, with the proliferation of overbearing machines that dwarf humanity and dominate the terrain of the CBD in sinister fashion.

I have been waiting for the invention of earthquake-related cocktails. Perhaps a competition could be run by the breweries to come up with a name and palatable drink, for instance 7.1, Crane Driver, Gerry or Clipboard cocktails; a Silver Lining sauvignon; a non-alcoholic High Viz fizz; a Liquefaction ale.

It is with sadness that I note that the old Rangiora Town Hall is to be demolished. I remember as a child whiling away many a happy hour raining Jaffas and Snifters upon the heads of those downstairs when the projector broke down and we kids had to wait impatiently while the projectionist dashed off to Kaiapoi to borrow a machine so normal transmission could be resumed as soon as possible.

I mourn for the days when picture theatres came with immense swathed curtains upon which different colours were flashed, before the curtains lifted or parted and we all stood for 'God Save the Queen'. Such deference to royalty seems absurd now but I well remember the sensation of my mother's rough careworn hand gripping me by the scruff of the neck and forcing me to stand. I suppose she, born three years before Liz I, was heavily under the influence of the virtuous monarch who gave up so much for the throne. My mother's children divorced about the same time as the queen's. When pot-stirrers would enquire about the splits, she would pipe up with the classy rejoinder, 'Actually, they make me feel very royal.'

Life after people

JANUARY 30 – Recently a friend's daughter returned for the first time since the February grand mal to her rented digs in Peterborough Street to salvage her belongings and was more than a little alarmed to notice that all the walls in the house were splattered in a ghoulish red.

Being a responsible citizen she immediately rang the police, who were terribly amused to discover on close inspection that the red stuff squirted across the walls was tomato sauce, not blood from a murder most foul.

Tomato sauce notwithstanding, it continues to amaze how quickly abandoned properties are reclaimed not by squatters or the government but by that seriously underestimated overlady Mother Nature. The visuals in the city are reminiscent of the documentary series *Life After People*, which showed grim part-fiction, part-natural science, sped-up scenarios of how quickly the planet would revert without humans.

A former resident of Christchurch who quit these shores years before the quake returned to visit family and called the mood of the city a post-apocalyptic dystopia, where those with damaged properties, floundering and unable to move on, can only vent their frustrations.

With the 'No Pay Rise for Marryatt' protest still scheduled for Wednesday and thousands predicted to turn up, one wonders if Tony Marryatt, the Christchurch City Council CEO who has for the most part failed to front, preferring instead to hide behind Sideshow Bob, will put in an appearance or leave the mayor to mouth the management platitudes.

Pushed into a tight corner, Marryatt has begrudgingly said no thanks to the pay rise, but it is too late for the hang 'em high mob; Marryatt and the mayor need more than the mayoress's thigh-length boots and a golf club to defend themselves from the well-deserved kicks. Who knows how it will end? Will democracy die in a day, or be given another chance in early autumn elections? Will the Bob & Tony Show leave town with the street performers from the World Buskers Festival?

I get talking to a man servicing one of the many coffee vans parked up at strategic points around the Red Zone offering caffeine fixes to the workers. He tells me that his sister-in-law, who has a rented property with damages that need fixing, has had to negotiate with the tenant, who has a long lease and wants $350 a day for the inconvenience. Then there are others whose landlords refuse to do any maintenance at all on houses with broken windows that need at least boarding up, telling them to wait until EQC eventually turns up. The turn-to-custard is pretty swift when people fail to exercise goodwill and common sense and cut each other slack.

My brother the vicar and I share a last meal together on his final night in town before he leaves to take up a new parish in Dunedin. His belongings have been in storage since February when his flat was torpedoed by Old Bucky so he is saved the slog of packing up, and just has to wait for the carriers to pick up his stuff and move it south. I'll miss him handing on novels he thinks I may enjoy, and our debriefs conducted in Bowronese, which only family members who have done time together understand. You know your parents for possibly half their lives if you're lucky, but you know your siblings right from day one, according to the order in which you rolled off the assembly line.

A few nights ago Jenny, who works for a local community organisation, kindly phoned to say that Joseph, the old guy about whom I have written a few times, died last Tuesday morning. His poor old chest, heaving with pneumonia, got the better of him and he expired two months short of the milestone he had hoped to reach, his ninety-fourth birthday. I went around to the boarding house where he lived to see if his fellow residents know of his passing and, yes, they had been informed.

As Joe requested, there will be no funeral, no full stop to celebrate his long life, but there are plans for a few of us to meet up later and do something with his ashes. One of the men at the boarding house said that Joe, who was made a ward of the state at a young age, was gifted at chasing people away.

When Joe and I first met I asked him what he thought about as he spent long hours sitting at the table staring out the window. He replied, 'Dreamtime.' The old soldier likened the June 13 quake to the barrage of Alamein, when 180 guns went off at the same time and he watched the water shimmer all the way to Alexandria from the percussion. I wonder if that's what it felt like as he quit the coil.

'All you've got is your memories,' he once told me, as he did his best to slip out the back quietly without anybody noticing, on his way to Dreamtime. But we will remember him.

Revolting peasants

FEBRUARY 6 – So Murray Lynch's anti-Tony Marryatt pay rise protest and call for early council elections was a lynch mob, according to some critics of the peaceful demonstration held last Wednesday. Actually it's a long time since I've witnessed a protest so across-the-board, the middle class standing shoulder to shoulder with a small contingent of the young and the restless.

Back in 1981 I marched through the streets of Christchurch to protest against the Springbok tour in a demonstration led by the bishop of Christchurch. Thirty years later, in a city notoriously shy of protest, the crowd were for the main part ratepayers. The police, in a low-key presence, didn't wield batons, and the spiritual leader was a former Baptist minister turned Anglican priest. Remember the term 'moral certainty'? Those who were so determined to get to a rally organised mid week in a worker-depleted CBD were saying loud and clear that they were more au fait with a reality called immoral uncertainty.

Stan, a well-dressed elderly man a year off ninety, had travelled specially in all the way from Yaldhurst Road. He told me he'd come along to stand up for open council governance and confessed it was the first time he'd joined 'rent a mob'.

If somebody could invent a reliable way of estimating crowds it would be much appreciated. On the day of the protest Radio New Zealand estimated the crowd at noon at 1,000, then updated it to 2,000. *National Business Review* estimated it, as I would have, at around 3,000, and *The Sunday Star-Times* put the rally at 4,000. The numbers game is important because in the days before the protest Mayor Bob Parker did his best to downplay the protest and have the media believe only a disaffected few hundred would attend. He must have convinced media north because, although there was a strong presence from media south, there was a no-show from television's major-domos – *Close Up*'s Mark Sainsbury and *Campbell Live*'s John Campbell.

Campbell Live did, however, pick up on the most poignant speaker at the rally, a fireman who contrasted Marryatt's insistence that his salary was hard-earned with his own work assisting an amputation at the PGC building after the February quake, carried out with a hacksaw and penknife. The fireman's annual salary was less than the CEO's controversial $68,000 pay rise.

It is easy for outsiders to think the Christchurch City Council is just another dysfunctional council, and that quake-traumatised and exhausted Cantabrians are just going through the last stages of a natural disaster phase, where there is discord and conflict between residents, council, government, and recovery providers. However, the mainly grey- and white-haired protesters filling the building-cleared vacant lot outside the council's Hereford Street premises are part of a growing revolution by people sick and tired of a narcissistic management ruling class that mouths jargon and platitudes instead of providing vision, swift commonsense solutions, and leadership.

Mayor Parker, who was on the way out before the last elections, has been both saved and destroyed by the intervention of the quakes. Although he is gifted at trotting out coherent and comforting platitudes, residents are now seeing through his blarney and disgusted at his desertion of post for ten days with his wife (whom he has called 'the most beautiful mayoress in the world') to drum up tourism in Asia. It beggars belief that he knew of the trip months earlier but didn't have the political nous to hand it over to one of his councillors. Not only did he misread the mood of his people, he also left his other half, the media-elusive Marryatt, without a mouthpiece to defend him from his own worst enemy, himself.

It seems too much to expect that Parker will see the light and mend his ways, but it would be a disaster for Cantabrians, already bristling under the yoke of CERA, to be further left out of the process with the introduction of commissioners. Reverend Mike Coleman said that out of the rally a movement

– Canterbury Unite – had been born, and called for an early autumn election for a new mayor and council. The government is against an early election as it would set an historical precedent and give those elected a longer term in power, but surely it is better to take the people with you than move in and shut them down? Such an action would most certainly turn Christchurch, newly minted blue, if not red then definitely less blue. One thing is for sure: the next council elections, whenever they are, will see a record number of residents exercising their franchise at the ballot box.

Coffee klatches

FEBRUARY 13 – Even though the summer has taken a turn for the worse and the cardigans are out in force, inside this bunker the carpet is pockmarked with great drifts of Benecine fur, as if it were the start of the moulting season. Perhaps it's the aftershocks, or maybe the old boy is getting old and neurotic, but I have never known an animal to shed so much fur. Honestly, I could sell tickets to a fur ball there's so much fluff clogged in his brush and comb, not to mention the wheezing stomach of the long-suffering vacuum cleaner.

Hardly a night goes by when I am not awakened by the noise of loud vomiting, groggily switch on the light, locate the small pool of fur-lined vomit, and clean it up before I place my bare feet on the floor. Yuk. It's not fleas but I'd better get him to the vet or Social Welfare will be on to me.

Families tend to belong in either a cat or a dog camp and early on my mother persuaded my canine-loving father to

Coffee klatches

become a card-carrying member of the feline fan club. I remember watching our first family cat, the imaginatively named Socks, dig a hole, make his deposit, then drag a delicate paw over the earth to tidily cover his waste product as my mother marvelled at his high standard of hygiene, always reminding us how much cleaner cats were than evil dirty dogs. I like both species, have had both, but seem to have ended up with more cats than dogs as they defect to me like Russian ballet dancers and I'm just a girl who can't say no.

While we're on the subject of excrement, it occurred to me the other day on a stroll around the neighbourhood that I hadn't seen dog poo on the streets for many moons, leading me to suspect that dogs have begun using the portaloos or, more likely, are taking advantage of the many abandoned properties in which to perform their wretched ablutions.

How wonderful it is to visit the Lyttelton farmers market on Saturday morning and observe that the place is again teeming with patrons and see every different style and hue of dog tied up at the entrance, all loitering together in peaceful coexistence. On the way over I was hurtling down Bridle Path Road and slammed on the brakes when I saw that Upshot Coffee, which used to be located in Heathcote before getting munted in the big February smack, has reinvented itself next to the riding school: you can put in your coffee order and stroll over to the stables to watch the ponies being saddled up and made ready for their small jockeys.

Every man and his dog were out in force to show support. A few chairs and old school desks lay about the yard and everybody seemed relaxed and dead chuffed to have their local up and running again. You don't need much, do you? Just a gathering point to show willing, which is also the case with Ground Culinary Centre, relocated to the Lyttelton Naval Point Club, where you can walk through the club dining room and out on to a deck with a fabulous view of the harbour that makes the other side seem so close you could reach out and touch it.

What a blow to hear the dismal news that several shops in Merivale Mall are temporarily out of action after being found to be an earthquake risk. Just when you think things are getting back to normal the hand of fate and quake knocks you back down on the mat. The saying 'It's not how many times you get knocked down, it's how many times you get back up' is the harsh and challenging reality for so many exhausted Cantabrians, who just want to put their shingles out and do the business.

The cold weather almost prohibited an excursion to the Botanic Gardens to watch the extremely funny *The Complete History of Christchurch (Abridged)*, in which three local actors possessed with so much boundless energy it should be hooked up to the national grid did everything they could to reduce the audience to howling wrecks. Mayor Bob Parker's infamous jacket put in an appearance, as did a rotund object called The Brownlee, while the sun obliged by coming out. One wondered how the mayor's clown workshop was going down overseas. It seems hard to believe that it will very soon be a year since you know what.

A chance to find the sunshine

FEBRUARY 20 – Only two more sleeps until February 22, and everyone I know is exhibiting some form of premenstrual tension before the arrival of the dreaded anniversary. It's like the build-up season in Darwin but without the humidity.

I hear a lot of people are clearing out of Christchurch for the day and with good reason. Of all the big shakes, two have occurred close to the significant date of Christmas and the thought of Old Bucky dishing out another smack on or around the anniversary is too much to bear.

I have declined invitations to dodge Dodge – as in leave town for the day – because for me it would just feel wrong to be in absentia. After all isn't this what calendars are for, to mark major events in our lives and remember the dead?

A few days ago I visited my parents' grave on the anniversary of my father's death and winced at the wasteland where they have fetched up. The lovely church and hall have been demolished, leaving only an office, the graves, and the ubiquitous post-demolition vista of ugly gravel. What I liked so much about Holy Trinity was the way the bone yard snuggled up to the church, but now with the building removed, wiped off the face of the Earth, it all seems rather pointless.

The rational part of me says: What does it matter? They're dead and gone and a long time looking at the lid. But Mum would be appalled at the aesthetic crime scene, while Dad would probably wax philosophical about the cacophony of bulldozers during the demolition, remarking there appeared to be 'no rest for the wicked'.

Seeing Sam Johnson, resplendent in dinner suit, on the front page of *The Press* after being crowned Young New Zealander of the Year was a welcome feel-good story in a newspaper that has had to be the bearer of so much bad news. When my mother died, Sam's aunt, a dear friend of mine domiciled in Australia, sent her nephew along to the funeral to represent her. I had just blithered out of the church at the end of the service when this lovely young man with a halo of angelic hair, pushing an elderly lady in a wheelchair whom he'd never met before, made himself known to me, telling me he'd even made notes on the eulogies to relay back to his aunt. All this happened pre quakes so I am happy to inform you, although it's hardly necessary, that our hero is the real deal, the genuine article, brimful of manners and blessed with a deep instinct for the right thing to do.

A chance to find the sunshine

When his aunt Jenny and I lived in Sydney, along with a bunch of other expat Cantabrians, if one of us had performed something DIYish or made something 'just like a bought one', we would describe the feat as being 'Canterbury-capable' – taking the Michael, but we knew what we meant. These days, when I am burdened with what seems to be a herculean task that phrase often springs to mind, encouraging the belief that because of that ace in the pocket, Canterbury capability, the job can be done. Sure that sounds terribly parochial, but hey, we'll take any advantage we can get these days.

The last year has challenged us, turned us She'll Be Righters into a Once Were Worriers' tribe. We will be holding our collective breath on the big Wednesday, waiting to let it out on the other side. This is the first anniversary and we have no idea how we will cope as we take stock, ponder all we've been through, and try and arrange our faces as the rest of the country observes us commemorating the day.

This big emotional stuff comes upon us at a time when the wounds have not healed as the aftershocks continue to knock the scab off again and again, pushing the healing game back to square one, and into the purgatory realm of Groundhog Day. The one thing we know is that things are different now – that *we* are different now, that we've lived through our own disaster movie but still don't know how it will end. As Maureen McGovern sang in *The Poseidon Adventure,* 'There's got to be a morning after / If we can hold on through the night.'

AWA PRESS

MORE BOOKS BY CHRISTCHURCH AUTHORS

So Brilliantly Clever: Parker, Hulme and The Murder that Shocked the World
Peter Graham

Beautifully written and wryly expressed … Not just about a murder but a revealing study of Christchurch six decades ago
– Willie Young, *The Press*

The Parker–Hulme case inspired Peter Jackson's award-winning movie *Heavenly Creatures* and remains one of the world's most shocking murders. Peter Graham tells the whole story – analysing the teenage killers using modern psychology, describing the ensuing trial, and providing a riveting account of the girls' strange lives since their release from prison.

ISBN 978-0-9582750-3-3

How to Look at a Painting
Justin Paton

Among the many things Paton does brilliantly is make art accessible to everyone
– Kim Knight, *Sunday Star-Times*

Justin Paton, an art writer and curator, takes the reader on a journey of exploration through the centuries and across the painted world. A premium best-seller, this book is an enduring classic and in 2011 was adapted as an acclaimed 12-part television series narrated by the author, who was awarded the 2012 Katherine Mansfield Menton Fellowship.

ISBN 978-0-9582538-8-8

**Available from all good bookstores
and online at www.awapress.com**